Systemize you~~r~~
your team, and leave a legacy

THE 2 DAY
CEO

SKYLAR LEWIS

TABLE OF CONTENTS

INTRODUCTION

I grew up wanting financial independence and freedom in my life. I believed I would get this freedom by becoming a business owner. I later discovered that most business owners are chained to their businesses; they can't get away physically, mentally, or emotionally. Their friends with "regular" jobs are more present at home with their families than they are.

Through many years of working with the world's top coaches and through my own business experiences, I finally found the answers. The 2-Day-CEO shares the exact strategies that took me from being financially bankrupt and chained to my business, to living a life of liberty through empowering my team.

This book is not for everyone. It is specifically designed to help business owners and their teams scale their companies while staying balanced in their lives. Many people reading this book will either be a CEO, manager or in a leadership role.

I started my entrepreneurial journey at the age of 10. I remember getting my first business cards made with my company name on them: Little Feet Inc. I would go door to door asking people in our neighborhood if I could clean their houses or do their yard work. Before I graduated high school I delved into a series of different businesses, including installing car stereos, website design, phone service deregulation, spray tanning, and high school candy distribution.

After high school I continued with several other businesses, and I was 23 when I became the CEO of my first million-dollar marketing company. Fast forward to today. I am the CEO of multiple multi-million-dollar companies, one being an eight-figure company with many team members. I have come into the office less than two days a week for over five years to efficiently accomplish my role as CEO. My business is located in California, and I recently moved to Dallas, Texas to run the $10 million dollar service-based business remotely. That business continues to thrive with only a couple of hours of my involvement virtually each week. My outcome is to support other entrepreneurs who have a vision of operating their business in less time with more results.

How can I be a 2-day-CEO? Our people run the company, and I have learned how to empower them to do it much better than me. This book is all about my real-world journey to getting to two days a week and the lessons I've learned along the way. There are proven systems and certain key strategies discussed in this book that make it all work.

As I am writing this book, I am in Austin, Texas, on day 28 of a 30-day road trip across the country with my family. COVID-19 has just shut down the entire world, and our workforce is temporarily remote. I thought it would be a good time to pack up and travel the country with my wife and our two boys. So, we loaded up our RV and visited 24 states. This trip has been one of the best experiences of my life, and I would not trade it for anything. I received only two work phone calls during this entire trip, which means I was able to be fully present with my family. While I was gone, the business had our best sales and production months ever.

In other words, I can be removed from my business and the business can scale and even become more profitable. Over the last two years, our team has increased profits an average of 45% each year!

I tell you this to share with you what is possible when you intentionally build your business as if it were a machine—a machine that will not only create freedom for you and your family, but also for your team members. The less chaos there is within your machine, the easier your team members' jobs and lives will be. I am so grateful when my team members take extended vacations, and the company still runs smoothly without them present. The only way that could happen is by building a systemized machine in every department.

THE 2-DAY-CEO

You may have read the title of this book and thought, "But I want to work five days a week. I enjoy working."

Just because you are only needed one or two days a week in your business does not mean you are limited to that. You can choose to work seven days a week. The goal is to be able to spend your time *where you want* to spend your time. Elon Musk has done this well and is now building rockets. Jeff Bezos is building… rockets. You don't have to build rockets, but you may have other great ideas that could be impactful for you, your family, or the world. Or what if you were able to expand your business 10x because you worked *on* the business (vision, strategy, exponential growth ideas), instead of being involved *in* the day-to-day tasks?

Having a business that operates without you generates results like:

- More time to spend with your family. I have been able to take month-long road trips, take weekends off for the last five years and stop working at 5pm during the week.

- Have happier team members. My team members now operate my company and make almost all the decisions. Their happiness and fulfillment from work has increased significantly.

- Being 100% present during the time you dedicate to your family. It means you are not a slave to your phone.

- Focus on some of your other passions. I love helping others, so I coach and support multiple non-profits.

- More income, profit, and wealth for you and your family.

- More energy and passion in life, which will lead to even more compounded success.

Is it possible?

YES. Period. Many of the world's top businesses are not operated by the owner/founder. Is Richard Branson dealing with airline pricing and staff issues? No, he is on his private island, and he is also… building rockets.

Founders are typically visionaries and may not be the best people to be operating the business. Therefore, you should be strategically planning to get yourself out of the business and moving towards the CEO role. Your focus should be on the vision and strategy of the company, which your capable and talented team would then execute.

Just because it is possible does not mean it will happen without diligent effort. It took me several years to develop and execute these strategies. Many business owners may never do what it takes to be free from their business. It is often because they don't think it is possible, and therefore they don't intentionally build their business with that end in mind. They also do not have mentors or teachers to show them the path.

Will it work with my business/industry?

Of course! Any business can be systemized. This is an objection I often get from attendees at my events. Let me give you some context. I am in the emergency water and fire restoration business. We get emergency calls 24/7 that are urgent and important. Some of these jobs are $100,000 to $1,000,000 projects that require extreme detail and skill to complete.

Some projects take over a year to finish. We have three separate divisions that operate independently and therefore require three unique sets of roles and processes. Our business is considered a complex, people-heavy business, but it was still able to be effectively systemized. Any business can be systemized. Let me repeat that again: *any business can be systemized.*

What will my team members think?

Early on, I had a fear that my team would be upset if I only worked a couple of days in my business. I was also concerned the team would slack off if I wasn't there. These fears caused me to build the business around ME. Team members needed to come through me to make all key decisions. This is what most business owners do.

What I realized was that when I had the right people, they wanted to run the business as opposed to always being told what to do. They craved the responsibility and fulfillment that came from making key business decisions. They really did not care that I was not always in the office.

Part of making this process successful is to hire the right people and communicate your role effectively. My team knows that I have invested significant time, effort, and money into the business, and I have risked a lot to get it to where it is. They also understand that they have a unique opportunity to be involved in a company that is employee-run.

Which option do you think your team would prefer:

1. An owner who is micromanaging them and directing their decisions on a day-to-day basis.

2. An owner who has given them the tools and resources to grow the business, and therefore have the autonomy to make the important decisions—and a chance to participate financially in the success of the company.

By not giving up the reins, you are preventing your team members from realizing their potential in their roles and lives.

What will I do with my free time?

The life of liberty that God has allowed me to live has given me the space to launch a company that is in direct alignment with my life's purpose, Rise Up Kings.

What are you most passionate about? What would you love to do every day?

While my businesses are certainly important and have blessed my life tremendously, they are not the most important things in my life. In fact, that word *'thing'* carries very little weight for me. It is the precious people in my life that are most important, and at the top of that list is God, my beautiful wife Jessica, and my two boys, Brenden and Jeremiah.

This life of efficiently running my businesses (rather than them running me) gives me the flexibility to spend the quality time I want with the people I love. It also opens up the brain space for me to be totally present when we are together. Far too often people may be with their family, but they are somewhere else mentally because their brains are full of other things. Someone once commented—and it makes perfect sense to me now—that the way you spell *love* is T-I-M-E.

In the end, it will not matter how many things we have acquired. What will matter will be the quality of time we have spent with the ones we love, and who we end up becoming.

This book will be a self-evaluation resource for both your personal and professional life, in whatever capacity you find yourself. I have included an opportunity at the end of most of the chapters to do a review and self-evaluation of the lessons learned as they pertain to your own life.

In addition, this book will provide you with inspiration, tools, strategies, and systems to significantly improve the efficiency of your life and business. If your title is CEO, fantastic. If you are a leader with a different title, wonderful. Either way, the principles and systems in this book will help you accomplish its vision, which is:

To inspire people to create a life of liberty and fulfillment through building their lives and businesses on purpose.

This is not meant to be a dry business book. I have purposely created *The 2-Day-CEO* to be a story that will take you through an intriguing journey, which happens to be my journey. I have added some fictional parts; however, the experiences threaded throughout this book are based on actual events in my life. I have changed the names of people throughout this book out of respect for their privacy.

This book has two core parts. The first outlines my journey to two days a week, and the second breaks down the specific tactics and strategies that I've used to get there.

That being said . . . let the journey begin!

PART ONE

THE JOURNEY

I was only 15 years old when it all started. I was a fairly above-average student in school, but—perhaps like other boys—my mind seemed to drift a bit when it came to focusing on the task in front of me. It wasn't that I wasn't paying attention in class; it was just that there might have been something more interesting to think about other than the school lesson. Although when we were doing something that really piqued my interest, I was ALL IN with laser focus. So, when the opportunity—or more like the dare—presented itself to sneak into a small restaurant in our town while it was closed, I guess you could say I was interested in the task at hand.

My life's experience up to that point just was what it was, and I didn't think I was any different than any other kid my age—although looking back, I definitely recognize how my circumstances shaped me to want something more out of life. At the age of four, my parents decided to get a divorce, which was confusing for my younger sister and me. Why any mother and father would not want to be together anymore made no sense to us. We lived in a 700-square-foot house that was what people might call "on the other side of the tracks". It was too small for all three of us to live in, so I actually slept in a free-standing shed in the backyard.

I guess I didn't know any different, and I was grateful to have a roof over my head. It also seemed sturdier than the single-wide trailer we had moved from, so for me, it was a step up in the world.

My childhood home.

A Fateful Night

There was a restaurant within walking distance that my buddies and I frequently visited called Ocatillo's. We would put all our money together to get one item on the menu. It was on one of these occasions while eating there that our adventurous adolescent minds came up with a plan to enter the restaurant late at night after everyone had left. Why? Maybe it was the thought that we could make ourselves a free meal; perhaps it was the peer pressure from my friends; perhaps we had an interest in checking out the stereo and band equipment on the small stage used for the weekend karaoke nights. Either way, it was summertime, and my friends and I were bored.

The night arrived for restaurant espionage by three teenage boys.

The Ocatillo roof was our late-night hangout that we visited when we had nothing to do. We had previously identified an unlocked hatch door on the roof that led down into the back storage room. That would be our entry point. There was a large tree close to the back corner of the building that easily facilitated my ascent to the roof.

Once on the roof, a thrill of excitement coupled with a bit of terror at the idea of getting caught went through my body. David and Josh both climbed up and joined me. We walked around feeling like we owned the restaurant and enjoyed the view.

"Check out these air conditioners," David said as he pointed to the commercial AC units. "You can get high off the chemicals inside them."

David pulled out a screwdriver, bent over, and started releasing the chemical from the unit. Little did we know that the chemical, freon, was incredibly toxic.

Suddenly, Josh screamed with terror as he noticed flashing lights. "It's the cops, let's get out of here!"

Josh immediately jumped onto the tree and climbed down. David hopped to his feet but fumbled to the ground, trying to recover from the freon intake. I quickly helped him up and guided him down the tree.

David and Josh got on their bikes and started furiously peddling away. My bike was parked in a different area than theirs so I made a run for it.

A police officer noticed me bolting from the back of the restaurant and yelled, "Hey, stop right there, don't move!"

What I heard was, "Hey, get the heck out of here and run as fast as you can!" Before I knew it, the officer was chasing me. I made my way to an empty parking lot, thinking I could hop over the block wall leading into a neighborhood.

It didn't turn out that way. The cop was a lot faster than I thought, because all of a sudden he was a short distance behind me with his gun pointed in my direction.

"Stop right there! Put your hands in the air!" The officer shouted with a voice that actually sounded like a gunshot.

I was paralyzed by the sound of his voice, and the knowledge that there was a gun pointed in my direction, so I did as he commanded. It was just like you see in one of those crime movies. I was handcuffed, read my rights, and led back to the restaurant in shame while some curious onlookers from across the street watched.

Once back at the restaurant, I was placed in the back of the police car with my hands cuffed behind my back, and the officer said, "I'll be back in a few minutes."

I immediately felt nauseous and completely humiliated at the thought of my family learning what I had done. My life as an upstanding citizen was over. I noticed the officer making a short phone call. Pretty soon he was back in the front seat of his cop car, but we were not moving. Then he asked, "What were you thinking, breaking into this restaurant like that?"

I remembered he'd told me I had the right to remain silent, but I decided to answer anyway. "We weren't really thinking straight. Are you going to put me in jail?"

"Hold on, did you say we? Were there others with you in there?" The observant officer asked.

Realizing I was in danger of throwing my friends under the bus, I decided to exercise my right to remain silent, and did not answer the officer's question.

After a few minutes of silence, the police officer said, "No, I am not going to put you in jail—yet. I know the owner of this restaurant, and called him to come down here. It will be up to him if he wants to press charges or not."

About 10 minutes later, a fancy car pulled into the parking lot, and the police officer got out of his car to greet the man whom I assumed was the owner of the restaurant. Watching from the car window, I saw the officer point in my direction while likely explaining what had happened. I noticed the owner shook his head and chuckled a bit, which I thought was odd, to laugh at a moment like this. Suddenly, the officer was making his way back to his car where he opened my door.

"The owner would like to speak with you. Get out of the car," he said in an unmerciful tone, and he led me, still handcuffed, to where the owner was standing.

"It's okay, Bill. Just give me a minute alone with him, if you don't mind. I'll let you know where we go from here," the man said to the police officer.

The officer made his way back to his car, and now I stood alone, facing this man whose intentions were a mystery to me, with my hands still locked behind my back. I was too embarrassed to look up or even make eye contact. A million thoughts were racing through my head while this well-built, fairly young-looking man folded his arms, stared like a laser in my direction, and began to breathe deeply, contemplating what he would say.

"You know, I bet you are a curious boy with a lot of courage, because breaking into my restaurant takes a fair amount of both," the man started in. "Are you hurt at all?"

My eyes welled up with tears as I let my emotions get the best of me. The man's question expressed a compliment and concern if I was all right. I had expected something totally different to come out of his mouth. Finally, in a humble, choked-up voice I muttered, "Yeah, I'm okay."

"Do you live close by here?" he continued.

"Just up the street a ways," I muttered while looking down at the pavement, still too ashamed to make eye contact.

"Is there anything you would like to tell me, young man?" He said in a soothing and somewhat forgiving tone.

I sniffled and leaned my head down to wipe my nose on my shoulder. Finally I summoned the courage to look the man in the eyes and said, "I'm so sorry sir, I know I shouldn't have broken into your restaurant. It was a dumb decision, and I am really sorry. It was a bad choice."

"I was right about your courage, boy, because apologizing and admitting you have made a poor choice takes a lot of it. What is your name?"

I hesitated to tell the man my name, not knowing if that was going to be held against me in the court of law, as they said in the crime movies I had watched. Nonetheless, I felt like I owed it to him to at least confess my name.

"It's Skylar, Skylar Lewis," I admitted.

"Well, Skylar, thank you for telling me your name. My name is Joseph, but my friends call me Joe. I have a couple of options for you. Option 1 is you and I work out a deal that is fair to both of us without involving the law. Option 2 is I turn you over to Officer Bill over there and we press charges. Which option do you want to go with?"

"Wait, you are not going to press charges against me?" I responded in a hopeful tone.

"Not if you choose option 1. Otherwise, yes, I will press charges," Joe stated.

I glanced over at Officer Bill, who was leaning against his car with his arms folded and a smirk on his face that said he would be more than happy to take me down to the police station. Anything sounded better than option 2, although I was still a little nervous about what option 1 really meant.

"Option 1, please," I said, attempting to sound grateful that I was not being turned over to Officer Bill.

"Wise choice, young man!" Joe said as he gave a thumbs up to Officer Bill, letting him know I would not be his prisoner that night.

The policeman approached me and uncuffed my hands. "You know you're a lucky young man, right?"

"Yes sir," I said thinking of my good fortune of not having to go to jail. However, that is not what Officer Bill meant.

"I don't mean receiving a get-out-of-jail-free card, boy. I mean anyone who gets to spend some personal time with Joe is a very lucky individual. You listen to everything he has to tell you, you hear?"

"Yes sir," I said again, nodding my head to acknowledge what the police officer had said. He obviously knew and respected Joe. My curiosity was piqued.

I rubbed my wrists to ease the irritation on my skin from being handcuffed. Soon, Officer Bill was gone and I was left alone in the dark parking lot with Joe.

"Well then, I have a proposal for you, Skylar Lewis. The fact is, you did break into my restaurant illegally, and I don't really want to press charges or make a big deal about it. I see potential in you, son, so how about we find a creative way to have you perform some community service to pay off the debt?"

"Community . . . service?" I said in agony, as if he just sentenced me to life in prison.

My mind quickly jumped to David and Josh, who should also be benefactors of this community service opportunity, and yet were likely at home having a nice warm meal as if nothing had interrupted their innocent summer evening. My resentful thoughts were interrupted as Joe started to explain his big idea.

"I would like you to come and help my team at my restaurant two days a week for the rest of the summer. I want you there on Tuesdays and Thursdays from 10:30 a.m. until 6:30 p.m. You can check out the whole restaurant without breaking and entering. In fact, you will get an amazing view under the toilets, because you will be cleaning them. You'll also be able to eat anything you want on your breaks. I will check in with you in about 30 days and then again at the end of the summer. If everything goes well and my team says you were helpful and did your part, this whole incident will never be mentioned or thought of again. What do you say, do we have a deal?"

It all sounded too good to be true. Was I being let off the hook by just coming to work at this man's restaurant twice a week? "Yes we have a deal, thank you, sir! Joe, can I ask why you are doing this for me instead of pressing charges?"

"That's a fair question, Skylar. Some of my best team members have been people that I did not expect to perform as well as they did. *I am always looking for people who have been operating well below their potential because of the low standards set by the people around them.* It's something I practice as a CEO, and train our team members to do as well. I've gotten pretty good at identifying team members for my companies with great character traits and untapped potential. I can tell you have untapped potential, Skylar."

Joe continued, "So I had a choice when I first saw you handcuffed in our restaurant parking lot tonight. I could have harshly reprimanded you and pressed charges, or I could entertain the possibility that you just made a poor choice, and make you my friend. So, my new friend, Skylar Lewis, you should probably get back home so your parents don't worry about you. I'll make the arrangements with my restaurant team so they know you'll be there Thursday."

Joe extended his hand cordially toward me, and despite my insecurities, I gave him the best loyal handshake I could muster. I didn't feel it necessary to tell him that it was only my mom at home, and not both of my parents, nor the fact that I lived in a place that some might look down on.

"I won't let you down, sir!" I promised as I hopped on my bike.

"I believe that to be true, Skylar, and I am expecting only the best effort from you!" he concluded.

CHAPTER 1

A STANDARD OF EXCELLENCE

All the things that usually embarrassed me about our lowly neighborhood did not seem to bother me anymore, or at least for the moment. I found my mom sitting on our little couch with an empty bottle of wine on the table and the television blaring. Even that didn't discourage me. Someone had shown an interest in me and believed I had courage and potential. I imagined for a moment what it would be like to be a team member in Joe's company and feel special like this all the time. Surely if he treated me like this, he must treat everyone like this, and especially the people on his team.

When I told David and Josh what had happened, they didn't believe it. Their mouths hung wide open and almost in unison both said, "No way, dude!" Even though I had to perform some community service, I felt like my friends were a little envious.

I did as I was asked, and showed up the following week to Joe's restaurant ready to pay my debt. I was greeted at the entrance by a middle-aged gentleman named Alex, who I later learned was the team leader.

"Hello there, young man, you must be the amazing Skylar Lewis?" Alex said as if I were some famous person.

"Uh . . . yes sir, that's me," I hesitantly answered.

"Come inside and sit down in the dining room for a minute while we have a brief meeting before we get the restaurant opened," Alex instructed.

Once the whole team was seated in the dining room, Alex started in. "Thank you, everyone, for being here on time for another amazing day of serving people. I want to personally welcome our new team member for the rest of the summer, Skylar Lewis. Joe told me personally that he is a workhorse with a lot of potential."

Alex's kind words caught me a little off guard, and a sudden smile was painted on my face. Nothing was mentioned or implied that I was serving a community service sentence. I instantly wanted to live up to the expectation that was expressed, and although I was much younger than everyone else, his compliment caused me to feel like an equal on the team.

My mind drifted to a movie I had seen called Seabiscuit that had scenes filmed in my hometown of Hemet, California. Seabiscuit was the name of a horse who was a small and scrawny excuse for a racing horse, but had so much fight inside of him that he beat the best horses of his day. There was one particular scene where the owner of the prized racehorse was asked by a news reporter how his small skinny horse was beating the much larger and stronger horses. The owner's reply stuck with me.

"Well, I just think this horse has a lot of heart. He may have been down, but he wasn't out. He may have lost a few, but he didn't let it get to him.

I think I learned a lick or two from this little guy. Oh, and by the way, he doesn't know he's little. He thinks he's the biggest horse out there."

Wrapped up in the moment, I felt like Joe was the horse owner, Alex was the horse trainer, and I was Seabiscuit. Alex continued to speak, interrupting my heroic, thought-provoking analogy.

"All right, everyone, you know your duties and what has to be done. Skylar will work with the busboy team for now. Before we start, Candace, can you please share with our new team member what our standard is here?"

"We do everything with a standard of excellence!" Candace said excitedly, knowing exactly what Alex was referring to.

"And what does that mean, Michael?" Alex inquired of another team member.

"That means that the only acceptable effort is our best effort until the job is complete," Michael said with confidence.

"That's right. Awesome! Thank you, Candace and Michael. Now, let's have a successful day, everyone," Alex concluded as we all went to work.

My new busboy team and I cleaned every nook and cranny of that restaurant, and made sure the outside of the establishment was immaculate as well. Everyone seemed to know their role, and the team leader, Alex, showed confidence in and acceptance of our work after briefly inspecting it. It was as if Joe was there himself making sure everything was done 100% completely. However, he did not have to be, because we all wanted him to know he could trust us to get the job done with a standard of excellence.

Summer rolled on, and true to his word, Joe showed up to his restaurant after 30 days to check on my progress. It should not have surprised me that he came back like he said he would, but I guess there were several experiences in my life where adults I knew said they were going to do something and never followed through. I gained a higher level of trust and respect for Joe from this one simple gesture of integrity.

"Hello, Skylar, great to see you again! My team leader and team members are all very impressed with you and the effort you've made. Well done!" Joe praised.

"Thank you, sir. They're a great team to work with, and I've learned a lot. The chef team even let me do a little prep work a few times in the kitchen," I responded.

"You've learned a lot, have you?" Joe inquired.

"Yes sir, I have, and I'm looking forward to learning much more!" I responded enthusiastically.

"That's wonderful Skylar. Really impressive, actually. You really are a unique young man. Now be sure to apply what you've learned. We only have a few more weeks of summer, and then you'll be back at school. I expect you to finish strong to fulfill our agreement. Can I count on you?" Joe asked.

"Of course—I do everything with a standard of excellence," I replied with a smile.

Joe looked me in the eyes, pointed at me, and winked. "Yes you do, my friend, yes you do!"

I realized my time was coming to an end with Joe, and I wanted to ask him a couple questions about his business.

"Um . . . Joe, can I ask you a question before you go?" I asked with a hopeful tone in my voice.

"Of course, Skylar."

I started, "How can I learn to do what you do? I mean have my own business with my own team members?"

"That's not a typical question from a 15-year-old boy, Skylar. Why would you want to know that?" Joe asked.

"I've noticed how you run your business, and honestly, I've never met anyone like you. I'm curious to know how you have achieved so much at such a young age."

My question caused Joe to pause and remain silent for what seemed like a very long time. He appeared to be thinking something over in his mind. Then he said, "You know what, Skylar, come with me. You can take the rest of the day off. I want to take you somewhere."

Joe headed towards the back door of the restaurant, retrieved my bicycle, and put it inside the back door of his restaurant. Soon we were driving in his fancy car, and my eyes went wide looking at all the gadgets. The leather smell was luxurious and extremely comfortable. I had never been in such a nice car. While driving, he called his wife on his car phone and explained that we were coming to their house. His last words to her before we pulled into the garage were, "Karen, take the boys into our bedroom, and I'll come in and get you in a little bit."

The house was enormous, with fancy vaulted ceilings, and I figured you could fit my whole home inside the entryway. Down the hallway I noticed pictures of their family, which consisted of a mom, a dad, and two young boys. Based on the photos, they were obviously world travelers. I saw a map of the United States and pictures of each of the states they had visited as a family, which appeared to be most of them. They looked like a happy family that enjoyed spending a lot of time together.

"Please have a seat, Skylar." Joe directed me to their living room couch.

"This is a really nice house," I complimented.

"Thank you. Of all the houses we own, this is one of my favorites."

My thoughts danced around in my head. What kind of guy and family live in more than one house? One house costs a lot of money. I was starting to put it all together.

"Are you a professional baseball player, Joe? Cause I know they typically have a few houses."

Joe let out a hearty laugh while shaking his head. "No, Skylar, I'm a business owner and the CEO of a few companies. Do you know what a CEO is?"

I shook my head no.

"It is an acronym for Chief Executive Officer. Some might say I am the main leader or head honcho of the company. But I don't run my companies—our talented team members do."

Gaining more confidence, I asked, "What kind of companies are you the CEO of?"

"Great question, thank you for asking! You know, we never find the answers we need unless we ask questions. To answer your question–you obviously know about my restaurant. I also own a leadership development company, and my largest company is serving people by restoring and rebuilding their homes or places of business after a devastating fire or flood. What kind of business do you want to run when you get older, Skylar?"

"I'm only 15 years old, and I'm just trying to make it through the 10th grade next year," I answered with a little sarcasm. Then I continued, "How did you become a CEO, and do you think I could become one someday?"

Joe pressed his lips together, squinted his eyes a bit, and began to nod his head. "That's another great question. Learning to become not just a CEO, but a *great* CEO, has evolved for me over time. I am constantly reading, attending seminars, being coached, and learning as much as I possibly can. You seem really serious about learning from me, Skylar."

"Yes sir, it's been on my mind ever since we met. I want to learn everything I can from you," I admitted.

"Well then, this could be an interesting opportunity for both of us," Joe replied.

"What do you mean, Joe?" I questioned.

He continued, "I mean you want to know how I achieved the life I have, and I have never actually taught anyone how I did it. The fact is, I know exactly how I did it and what it takes so others could duplicate this process. So—I will show you, Skylar. I will show you what I've done to achieve what I have. Essentially, I will be your mentor."

I wasn't sure exactly what that meant, but it sounded good. I wanted to learn what Joe knew, but I also wanted to know what I was committing to. Joe saw the concern on my face and laughed. "That means we'll meet together throughout the summer, Skylar, and I'll start to teach you."

My eyes widened with excitement. "Really Joe, are you serious?!"

"I am very serious, Skylar. You have shown me a tremendous amount of commitment and coachability, and that's all I need to move forward. There are many people who think they are successful enough, and that's when they stop learning. They think they know it all. It prevents people from getting to the next level. I can tell you are hungry to learn, and I like working with people like that."

"Wow, thank you sir, when do we start?" I said, a little over-zealous.

"We will start this week. I will come visit you at the restaurant before your shift is done. Now, before you go, I would like you to see the treasures in my life. Please wait here a moment," Joe requested as he stood up and made his way down the hall.

As I watched this peculiar man walk away from me, my eyes widened with anticipation at what kind of treasures he was going to show me. I had never seen real diamonds or bars of real gold. Maybe he was going to show me some fancy watches?

While I was lost unburying Joe's treasures in my mind, I was interrupted by his voice. "Skylar, please meet my beautiful wife Karen and my two precious boys, Joey and Jeremy."

Karen approached me with her hand cordially extended. "It's a pleasure to meet you, Skylar. Joe explained that you have been a part of our restaurant team this summer. I am glad to hear that."

I was a bit taken back by her kindness, but nonetheless grateful that she, too, treated me like an immediate friend.

"C'mon boys, meet our new friend Skylar," Joe urged his two boys along.

"Hello Skylar, my name is Joey, and I am eight and a half years old," the taller boy said politely as he shook my hand.

"Hey Skylar, I'm Jeremy and I'm five, but I'm just as strong as Joey. My dad is 34!"

We all laughed at Jeremy's bubbly personality. I also understood very quickly that Joe's treasures had nothing to do with things, although I could see he had plenty of those as well. The important people in his life were his biggest gems.

After meeting Joe's amazing family, he gave me a ride back to his restaurant to retrieve my bicycle.

I rode my bike home as fast as my teenage legs could peddle with a huge smile glued on my face. I had just met a real CEO! Even though I did not fully understand what that meant yet, a desire inside of me was ignited like a raging bonfire to become just like Joe.

Once home, a simple yet profound realization dawned on me because of the way I was feeling and the way I had been treated by Joe. It was what my freshman English teacher called a lesson learned. She taught us to take time and write these lessons down every time we had one. I made my way to my personal shed in the backyard and took out the spiral notebook my mom had purchased for me from the dollar store designated for my sophomore year of high school. I found a black marker and wrote on the front cover *"Lessons Learned from The CEO."* With my favorite pen, I noted what I had learned so far.

LESSON #1: STANDARDS OF EXCELLENCE

People will rise up to the expectations and standards you set for them.
Hold high standards for yourself and your team members.

I could hardly wait for my first official visit with Joe at the restaurant. I felt a new focus and excitement about life. Soon enough I found myself sitting in the restaurant office with my Lessons Learned from The CEO notebook, ready to absorb everything he told me like a dry sponge begging for water.

"What's that you have there?" Joe asked, glancing down at the notebook in my hand.

"Oh, this is my Lessons Learned notebook. I have to write down everything I learn from you," I explained.

"I like that, Skylar. You will definitely gain a lot more by making the effort to write things down. It's a simple gesture, but it has a profound impact on a person's level of success and achievement!" Joe complimented enthusiastically.

Joe began by telling me some of his accolades in a humble manner in order to help me see what was possible. I learned that he had hired hundreds of team members, and his three companies produced millions upon millions of dollars in revenue–all while he worked only two days a week at his primary business. He lived an incredible life of liberty and fulfillment. He told me this required not just one strategy, but rather an accumulation of many things.

"Skylar, I will teach you how to do this over time. Just know that each one of your lessons learned, as you call them, will have a specific purpose to help you achieve what I have—hopefully even greater. In fact, let's start with the first lesson right now. You see that Bible on the bookshelf behind you? Can you hand it to me, please?" Joe politely asked.

I looked over at Joe and noticed a Bible sitting in his office. I grew up in a Christian household, but my parents did not really represent God well. My mom had often mentioned that wealthy people usually achieved their status by oppressing the poor, or something of the sort. It was refreshing to meet someone who was into God and had created an incredible lifestyle.

Joe started in again, "One of the first things I want you to know is the wrong way of doing business. For many years I operated out of selfishness. I was after the money, the feeling of significance because of my success, and the coveted title of CEO or president or owner. I didn't realize it, but my ego was very large; it was all about me. At some point, I recognized that my ambitions were in vain. I was making lots of money and working long hours, but I was unfulfilled."

"You see," Joe continued, "we are all creatures seeking fulfillment in some way, shape, or form. Oftentimes, men and women find their fulfillment in destructive habits, or from things that don't truly serve them. I have to admit, for a period of time I indulged in some pleasure-seeking until I became wiser."

"Once I recognized this about eight years ago, I made a big shift to operate for a higher purpose, which is to build a business that will make an impact by the way I treat my team members, my customers, my vendors, and my community. I can honestly say it is no longer all about me, and it feels amazing. When you operate from humility as opposed to ego, your life will be much more full. Interestingly enough, ever since I shifted my focus off of me and began to operate from a place of humility, my business has massively expanded with success."

Joe thought that was enough mentoring for now, and said we would meet again in a few weeks before the summer ended and I was back at school.

"Perfect. Thank you, Joe. I'll see you in a few weeks," I said as I returned to my duties in the restaurant.

Once home, I took out my *Lessons Learned* notebook to jot down more of what I'd gleaned from working with him that summer.

LESSON #2: LEAD WITH HUMILITY

Great leaders show up as servant-leaders to support the greater cause.
They treat their team members as equals and never talk down to them.
Team members need to feel like they work *with* the CEO, not *for* the CEO.

After noting down my lessons learned, I sat and pondered what I wanted my life to look like when I was in my mid-thirties like Joe. Up to this point in my life, I had never made it a practice to dream bigger than my current set of circumstances.

That changed when Joe said he would mentor me, a kid who came from a broken home and did not feel worthy of his mentorship. I felt the constant battle between two opposing forces start again in my head. On the one hand, I felt like I was as good as anyone else my age, I could accomplish anything, and was maybe even destined for greatness. On the other hand, there were constant reminders of my current reality staring me in the face, stifling any possibility of snapping the poverty chain and becoming a successful leader, husband, and father. Furthermore, nothing ever seemed to work out in my favor long-term. Somehow I had developed the destructive belief that if something was amazing, it would eventually be taken away from me.

For the moment, I blocked out the negative and unproductive thoughts and decided to focus only on the positive. So I began writing what I wanted my future life to be on the front inside cover of my notebook.

- I will be a successful CEO of a company with many team members that love working for me and want to follow me, just like Joe.
- I will have a hot wife with kids I spend time with.
- I will create a life of massive success by helping others.

REVIEW AND EVALUATIONS OF LESSONS LEARNED

LESSON #1: STANDARDS OF EXCELLENCE

People rise up to the expectations and standards you set for them. Hold high standards for yourself and your team members.

How well do you build up your team members and hold high standards?

Circle your current, honest answer.
1 = Not at All and 5 = Always.

I regularly encourage my team members with positivity.

| 1 | 2 | 3 | 4 | 5 |

I treat my team with trust and respect.

| 1 | 2 | 3 | 4 | 5 |

I build up my team members by believing they can do even better than they currently are.

| 1 | 2 | 3 | 4 | 5 |

For any answer below a 5, what specific actions can you take to improve?

_____

_____

_____

LESSON #2: LEAD WITH HUMILITY

Great leaders show up as servants to support the greater cause. They treat their team members as equals and never talk down to them. Team members need to feel like they work with the CEO, not for the CEO.

How well are you leading with humility in your organization? Circle your current, honest answer. 1 = Not at All and 5 = Always

I treat my team members as equals and never talk down to them.

1	2	3	4	5

My team feels like they work with me and not for me.

1	2	3	4	5

I show up as a servant-leader to support the greater cause.

1	2	3	4	5

For any answer below a 5, what specific actions can you take to improve?

_____

_____

_____

_____

Download the 360° leadership assessment from
www.2dayceo.com/resources

CHAPTER 2

CORE VALUES AND CULTURE

The summer rolled on, and the start of my sophomore year of school was approaching. One evening while eating some ramen noodles, I glanced at my worn-out mother. She was constantly working 12-hour shifts as a caregiver. She was doing everything she could to provide for us, and I felt it was time to help contribute to the family finances by finding a job.

I made my way to the shopping plaza that was fairly close to our house and set out to find employment that I could easily ride my bike to. There were a couple of fast-food restaurants, but I couldn't really see myself working at any of them. Then I found myself in front of the store that felt like the right fit: Smart & Final. It seemed like an easy job. They specialized in providing households and businesses with products in bulk. We never really shopped there, because we were not buying anything in bulk at my house except maybe boxed wine. I asked for an application, filled it out, and turned it in on the spot. I was told I needed to wait for them to call me for an interview if they were interested.

Waiting for that call from Smart & Final on our home landline and checking the answering machine at least five times a day might have seemed a little excessive, but I really wanted that job.

The summer's end was approaching, and I showed up for my last time to complete my community service at Joe's restaurant. I was once again grateful he was there to greet me as promised.

"Skylar, you have kept your word and have been very diligent in helping our team this summer. I'm satisfied with your efforts, and you have a clean record with me now. So what's next for you?" Joe asked.

"Well, I'm trying to get a job at Smart & Final to help out my family, but they haven't called me back yet," I explained in a hopeless tone.

Joe folded his arms and took in a deep breath. I knew whatever he said next was going to be important. "How serious are you about getting that job, Skylar?"

"I mean, pretty serious, I've waited for them to call me every day for almost two weeks now," I said, expecting some sympathy.

Joe paused again before speaking. "Skylar, if you really want that job, then go get that job instead of waiting for it to come to you. Go to that store and talk to the person in charge and let them know that you are serious about being hired."

"You mean just go down there without them calling me first?" I asked doubtfully.

"Exactly! That will leave an impression on them. And remember what I'm about to tell you for the rest of your life. It will make all the difference. Are you ready for it?" Joe said convincingly.

My ears perked up and my eyes were locked in, already committing in my mind to write down the lesson Joe was about to give me. "Yes sir, I am ready!"

Joe motioned for me to follow him and briskly walked through the restaurant. Soon we were both in the restaurant office, and before sitting down, he grabbed two bottles of cold water from the mini fridge and removed his laptop from his briefcase. He immediately opened his laptop and started searching for something. The restaurant team was busy preparing for another successful day, and the loud noises of pots and pans meeting metal cooking utensils coming from the kitchen sounded like a drumline. My mind wandered a bit as I looked at all the books he had stacked neatly on his office bookshelf.

Finally, Joe started in. "So, if you want that job—or any job, for that matter—you must show that you are aligned with their core values. I've learned the most successful companies hire and fire based on their core values. The more people that are on a team with similar core values, the more unified they become. Skylar, when you build your company, you'll want to get clear on the values that are most important to you and to the health and growth of your company."

Joe opened up his laptop and located the Smart & Final website. "Look here. Smart & Final's core values are teamwork, integrity, accountability, respect, and growth. I can attest, and you can even put me as a reference, that you possess these core values. Actually, this is the perfect time to share something else with you," Joe said.

Before long he had photocopied another piece of paper from his notebook. "Here, Skylar, this will come in handy right now for your job. Much of it will be used later when you have your own companies, but for now, I want you to read it over and apply what you can. Got it?" the CEO instructed.

I wasted no time and studied the information Joe had gifted me.

Why Core Values Are Important

Having a great culture is important in any organization, whether it is a church, a non-profit, a business, or a political organization. How do you build an intentional company culture that is most effective for a business that is run independently of you? A critical part of this is getting clear on your core values, and the other is having a process in place to make those core values become a part of the fiber of your company.

What is company culture?

Each leadership expert has a different definition of company culture. Here is mine: company culture is the shared core values and behaviors of people within an organization.

Core Values

Core values are the set standards that the people within your organization operate by. They are the company's DNA within you and your people. They dictate and are exemplified in the way team members communicate, treat others, and do their work. You do not "create" your core values. You uncover them. Being intentional with these core values is critical.

When I hired my first business consultant, one of the first things he did was a core value discovery exercise. He sat down with me and asked me about my personal values. Then he asked, "Based on company results, what are the company's values?" What great traits were already a part of our company that we wanted to instill into future team members? Once we got clear on a general idea of our values, we got together with our senior-level staff. We put them in a room and wrote on a whiteboard what they thought made our company unique. We brainstormed as many things as came to mind, then summed them up into categories, which led to our core values. These values, through time, became ingrained within every person in our organization. I suggest no more than five core values. Three to five is usually good.

What do you do with your core values?

Many companies miss this crucial component and do not have their core values clearly defined. If they do, oftentimes their team members do not know them. If you are going to create core values, it is important that you lead from the front by knowing them, and even more important, by living them. Then and only then can you rightfully expect your team to adopt and eventually live by them on a daily basis.

Here are some ways to get your team to embrace and "own" your core values:

- Have company-wide meetings and share the core values with the entire team. As upper management, it is important for you to share stories related to the core values.

- Have team members regularly share stories that represent the core values at weekly or monthly meetings. Ex: "I want to recognize Bobby for going above and beyond for a customer. He took out her trash cans because she was unable to do so."

- Any time you recognize a team member, find a way to relate it to a core value.

- Put the core values up on the wall, on team member badges, on email signatures, etc. Get creative.

- Dive deep into your core values during orientation meetings.

One of the most effective ways I have found to get buy-in from the entire team is to have the team members share stories of other team members they have seen utilizing the core values. Have a few people speak up about a team member they saw live out a core value. This really weaves the core values into the everyday work of the team members, which is exactly what you want. What you do not want is the core values to become stale, cold, and distant. The #1 way to bring them to life is to share stories and recognize when they are being applied.

Hiring, firing, and reviews based on core values

All new hires must live the core values. How do you know if a candidate possesses the core values? We utilize our core values during our interview process. We have structured questions that uncover whether the candidate has the core value or not. We make notes based on the questions and check off the core values once we are satisfied with their alignment.

We also measure team members' performance based on core values. How well is that team member showing mindfulness or collaboration? If we have issues with a team member not showing the core values, we coach them. If coaching does not work, they will eventually be terminated. Your team members must know that they need to live by the standard of the core values. They are that important. When you hear about companies with a poor culture, it is usually the result of management not holding team members accountable, or not taking the time and effort to coach those who are not living up to the core values.

What are your company's core values?

_____

_____

_____

_____

_____

How will you specifically implement these core values into your company?

Just then, someone knocked at the office door. "Come in," Joe promptly responded.

Alex, the team leader, came in to report on a business matter he had been entrusted with. Then Joe asked, "Alex, how is your son's baseball season going? Is he still working towards a college scholarship?"

"It's going great! He has four colleges already expressing interest in him. I'll let him know you were asking about him," Alex answered with a smile.

"Well, please give him my best wishes on another successful season," Joe said.

Then Alex went back to work, and I had to ask. "Joe, how did you know about Alex's son playing baseball?"

I figured the answer should be obvious, but I was a little taken aback that the owner of the company would know some intimate details about his team leader.

Joe started in, "It's pretty simple, really. When I'm with my team, I ask them to share their story with me. Things like why they applied to work with us, and what are their interests outside of work. It is also important that our team members know our company story, our *Why*."

"What do you mean, 'your *Why*'?" I asked, intrigued.

"I mean *why* do we do what we do in that particular business. This way, our team knows they are working for a cause and not just for the money. Also, on a personal level, I get to know their story so they feel more valued as a team member. As I grow my companies and I spend less time in the business, I mostly get to know the stories of my team leaders, and they get to know the stories of their team members. It would be wise for you to learn a little bit more about Smart & Final's story, and why they do what they do, before you go interview with them," Joe explained.

I was so grateful for all the gold nuggets of information Joe was freely sharing with me. He also gave me some pointers on how to communicate with confidence during the interview. Then Joe handed me his business card and said with a smile, "Now go get that job, and you call me on the phone number on this card to let me know the good news."

I raced home, cleaned up, and put on my best pair of church slacks, along with the only button-down shirt and tie I had. I wanted to review what Joe had told me before I went to get the job, so I took out my notebook and began to write what I could remember.

LESSON #3: HIRE BASED ON YOUR CORE VALUES

The most successful companies hire and fire in alignment with their core values.

LESSON #4: KNOW YOUR WHY

Make sure your team knows your company story and your *Why* (why you do what you do), so they are working for a cause and not just the money. Get to know your team members' personal stories so they feel valued.

Feeling satisfied with my lessons learned, I scurried outside for my bike. My younger sister, Adrianna, wondered why I was all dressed up and in such a hurry.

"Where are you going looking like that, Skylar? You have a hot date with another bike rider?" she wisecracked.

I glanced back and acknowledged her wittiness. "No, I am going to get a job right now!"

Upon arriving at Smart & Final, my demeanor was different. I walked into the place determined to work there. I was no longer a potential candidate for the job, I was The Candidate for the job. I made my way back to the store offices and asked to speak with the manager.

"Hi there, young man, I am the manager. How can I help you?" A gentleman greeted me who looked to be in his mid-forties.

"Thank you for your time, sir. I am Skylar Lewis. I submitted an application recently, and I wanted to see if you had a minute to interview me for the job."

"I see. Did someone call you to be interviewed?" the manager curiously inquired.

"I'm not sure if they called or not, but I've been diligently waiting for someone to call. So, I thought instead of just waiting around, I would take the initiative and show up. Also, after studying your core values of teamwork, integrity, accountability, respect and growth, I know I'm aligned perfectly with this company," I explained with confidence, but not arrogance.

The manager raised his left eyebrow and smiled without speaking. He sat down in his chair at his desk and started thumbing through a file cabinet. He finally pulled out a file folder marked "applications" and started sifting through what seemed like a hundred pieces of paper.

"Aha, here you are. Skylar Lewis, right? Please sit down," the manager beckoned.

I did my best to keep my composure, but my thoughts were a little giddy. Was this really happening? I was having an unannounced interview with the manager. I sat quietly, waiting respectfully for him to ask me a question.

"Skylar, my name is Chris. You have impressed me a bit, and after looking through your application, it seems you are qualified to work here. Can you please tell me why you want to work here, though?" he inquired.

I sat up straight in my chair and looked Chris square in the eyes, just like Joe told me to do when communicating in the interview. "Great question, sir. After learning about your history and how this company was started in 1871 in Los Angeles, and since has expanded to over 250 stores, I was captivated. The simple fact is I'm looking for work to help support my mom and younger sister, and it would be great to be part of a company with such deep heritage."

Chris paused for a bit, and I sat there a little nervous that maybe I hadn't said the right thing. He finally started in, "Wow, in all my years here, I have never heard a better answer than that, Skylar."

I must have impressed Chris, because he offered me the job and asked if I could start on Monday. I enthusiastically got on my bike at my new place of employment with a sense of accomplishment.

"I did it, I really did it! I did what Joe told me to do, and it worked!" I said with the distant coastal wind blowing in my face while no one was listening.

I was excited to tell Joe the good news, so the moment I arrived home I bolted for the phone. Just as I dialed, my sister entered and asked if I got the job. I winked at her and gave her a positive thumbs up, letting her know that I was now employed.

"Hello Joe! This is Skylar, Skylar Lewis!"

"Hi there, buddy, you sound excited. How did it go at . . .?" Joe attempted to inquire, but before he could finish, I had already started in.

"I got the job, Joe, I walked straight back to the manager's office and asked for an interview, and he hired me right on the spot. I start on Monday! Everything you said to do worked. He was super impressed with me, and that I knew the company's core values and history. Just wanted to call and thank you for your help!" I energetically explained.

"That's super, Skylar! I knew it would all work the way it was supposed to. I am proud of you!" Joe congratulated me.

I promised to keep Joe in the loop with my progression. The summer had been one to remember forever, one that would essentially change the course of my life. With The CEO as my inspiration, I was constantly thinking of ways to make money. Little did I know that this particular job and its wholesale benefits were going to perfectly facilitate a business for me.

The next few weeks went by quickly, and before I knew it, I was back at high school during the day and working at Smart & Final after school and on the weekends. One day after lunch, I noticed a line of kids at one of the school vending machines. I had never really noticed the machines or what was in them before, but as I got closer, I realized it was full of snacks. The next day, I observed the same thing at the same time–a line of students eager to get treats out of the vending machine. It was consistently in high demand. Eventually, I found myself in that same line, so I could get a good look inside of the machine and see what kind of items they were selling. Candy bars and larger items like Twinkies were $1.00, and a few smaller items, like Life Savers, were 50 cents.

The day came when a little something sweet sounded nice, so I indulged and bought a candy bar. I rationalized that now I had some extra cash on my hands from my job, and I could afford a little somethin' occasionally. That night at work, my duty was to stock the shelves. Halloween was approaching, so we had to make a whole new section just for the influx of candy and boxed snacks. As I placed the items on their shelves, I noticed the price tag. Suddenly a light bulb went off in my head. With my team-member discount, I could buy all these snacks and sell them at school! For me, a whole package of 12 brownies was only $4, and kids will pay a whole dollar for them individually. Our school was making a huge profit!

I recalled something Joe quoted over the summer: "You don't have to be great to start, but you have to start to be great." With that mentality, one night before we closed out the registers, I decided to start my sweet-treat-selling business. I purchased five packages which each had a dozen popular items in them, such as brownies, Little Debbie Cakes, and Twinkies. I asked the register clerk to give me twenty one-dollar bills so I would have change for my customers.

The next day before school, I loaded the treats in a duffle bag along with a zippered money pouch and went to work. I spread the word to anyone and everyone, and just after lunch time I sold 60 snacks on my first day. My net profit was $40. At my current pay rate, it would have taken me over five hours to make that same $40 at my job. Another light bulb went off. I could reinvest all of my gross profits into buying 15 packages of snacks, and after selling all those, my net profit would be $120 in a single day!

The plan worked like magic—for the most part, anyway. I bought 15 dozen snacks and sold them, although it took me almost three days to do it. I couldn't seem to get to enough places or customers to sell all of my inventory in one day like I wanted to. Our school had just over 3,000 students and I was just one guy.

Pretty soon, with this business model I was making four times the amount of money with my sweet-treat-selling business than I made at my Smart & Final job. I felt I had done something to be proud of and wanted to tell Joe, so one day after school I rode my bike over to his house, where he had taken me the night of the incident, hoping he would be there. Luckily, I got there just in the nick of time, as he was about to get in his car and leave.

"Hey, look who it is! How are you, my friend?" Joe said as he came over to give me a high five.

"Hi Joe, everything is going great! I came by hoping you were here because I wanted to share some exciting news about my new snack-selling business."

Joe folded his arms, began to smile, and said, "Wow Skylar! Sounds like a pretty sweet business. Tell me about it!"

I groaned at his intentional pun about the sweet business. I explained the details of how I purchased boxed items at a discount and then sold them to my fellow students for a profit. I also potentially bragged a little about how much more I was making selling snacks than I was at my real job.

"Great work, Skylar! That's certainly impressive. How long does it take you to get through your inventory?" Joe asked pointedly.

"I've been selling about 15 dozen items in about three to four days, on average," I proudly responded.

Figuring he was going to congratulate me, I rounded my shoulders and began to nod my head in the "that's right" motion when someone does something really brilliant. However, that was not the direction he was heading.

"Hmm, only 180 items in three to four days? And how many students are at your school?" Joe challenged.

A little taken aback, I fumbled to answer. "*Only* 180 items? But I'm working every angle I can to get students to buy. I'm not slacking off..."

"Skylar, I am not suggesting that you are slacking off. I'm simply looking at larger possibilities. I compare how many students are at your school to the number of items sold to evaluate the potential in the market. You have done a tremendous job by yourself," Joe reassured me. "Here is a mindset I live by: "*If you're going to set a goal, why not set a big one.* The way to achieve big success is by leveraging the help of others. Do you understand?" Joe's demeanor showed compassion, but the tone of his voice was still firm.

"Yes, I see what you are saying," I answered.

"So how many students are at your school?" Joe repeated.

"About 3,000," I replied.

Joe took out the calculator on his phone and began to work some numbers. He explained that I was capturing approximately 12% of the student market every three to four days, which was decent. However, he wondered what it would take to bump that up to 36%, or in other words, 3X my business.

"I am only one guy, Joe, and I only have a limited time to sell," I contested, with my narrow-minded understanding of Joe's theory.

"Exactly my point, young man! You are only one guy with a limited time to sell. That is why you need to hire a sales team to 3x your efforts! " Joe explained enthusiastically.

"Well, if I hire a sales team, I have to pay them, and there goes all of my profits," I protested.

"Let me help you understand better, Skylar, because your profits will dramatically increase with a sales team."

Joe took out a piece of paper and a pen from his car and began to draw it out for me. He showed three salespeople all selling 180 snacks in five days, or a whole school week. I would pay the sales team half of the profits. That would leave me with $60 net profit per week per sales person, which is $180 from my team plus the $120 net profit I earned from my own sales. So, with a team I would be making a total of $300 a week in net profits—almost three times what I made by myself.

Joe concluded with this powerful piece of knowledge. "The only way that I can live a life of true liberty is through empowering other people to do the work. This is called leveraging other's efforts and is a key aspect to really scaling any business exponentially. You cannot be everything to everyone; you must empower a team!"

Suddenly, the light turned on in my head, and I saw clearly how having a sales team to duplicate my efforts was like magic. I thanked Joe for the amazing insight and set out to find three snack distributors. That night I noted down my lesson learned from the CEO.

LESSON #5: EMPOWER YOUR TEAM

The best way to create a life of liberty and fulfillment is through working with others. Leveraging other's efforts is a key aspect to scaling a business exponentially. You cannot be everything to everyone; you must empower your team!

I didn't waste any time putting this lesson into action. Within a week I had hired a team of three freshmen, and we were ready for business. I didn't just hire anyone; I hired the best I could find. Each morning before school I would meet with them to refill their inventory, and they would give me the 50% split from their previous day's sales.

Remembering how Joe operated, I committed my sales team to operate with a standard of excellence. To me, this meant never quitting until we had sold all our daily inventory. We rolled along for several weeks, and I even started seeing a glimpse of how Joe felt as a CEO. I brought on additional distributors. I was surprised at how easy it was to make money. Until that one fateful day. . .

"Skylar Lewis, please report to the principal's office immediately, Skylar Lewis to the principal's office!" the school public announcement system blared out for everyone to hear.

Truth be told, this was not the first time I had been publicly summoned to the principal's office. It's not like I was a regular visitor or anything, but I knew that the summons were typically not for reasons of positive recognition, and this visit proved to be the same.

The scene was just like one would see in a high school movie. The principal's secretary says to the student, "Have a seat over there," and you sit on a hard chair and wait nervously for the principal. Finally, our principal came out of his office like a prison warden and called me in.

"Mr. Lewis, you might have an idea of why I called you in, but just in case you don't, this might help you understand," the principal said as he held up one of my freshman sales guy's bag of snacks.

I sat there waiting, a bit curious to see what the problem was, because I was not aware of any rules that said I could not sell snacks on campus. The principal continued, "It is not permissible, Mr. Lewis, to sell something on our campus that competes with products we are selling. We sell candy and similar snacks in our bookstore and vending machines, and have the proper licensing to do so. So, here is your bag of snacks, and we are officially placing a cease-and-desist order, or in other words an immediate stop order on your snack-selling business. Is that clearly understood, Mr. Lewis?"

"Yes sir, I understand. I apologize—honestly, I wasn't aware that I couldn't sell snacks on campus," I said, dejected.

After school, I met with my sales team to share the news that our business had been shut down. They had already anticipated it after they heard me being called to the principal's office. I expressed my thanks to them and gave them their final commission payments. While we could have continued selling off campus, I felt it was time to hang up the sweet-treat business. It was a good run, and a valuable lesson learned as well.

Riding my bike home, I tried to stay positive, but I was consumed by that negative force attacking me again. I couldn't get the pessimistic thoughts out of my head. *"See, I told you, nothing great ever works out for you long term! You will always find a way to mess it up. You will struggle all your life to make money. What girl would ever want to be with a man like that..."*

REVIEW AND EVALUATIONS OF LESSONS LEARNED

LESSON #3:

The most successful companies hire and fire in alignment with their core values.

Evaluate your current core values in your organization and personally.

My company has clear core values and I have them memorized.

Yes	No

(Examples: teamwork, integrity, accountability, respect and growth)

I have a list of personal core values.

Yes	No

Circle your current, honest answer.
1 = Not at All and 5 = Always

Our team members know and live by our core values.

1	2	3	4	5

If any of your answers are "No" or not at a 5, what specific action can you take to improve and what timeline will you set for yourself?

_____

_____

_____

LESSON #4:

Make sure your team knows your company story and your Why (why you do what you do) so they are working for a cause and not just for the money. Get to know your team members' personal stories.

Our organization has a company story and our "Why" is clear.

Yes   No

As the leader, I know my key team members' personal stories.

1   2   3   4   5

If your answer is "No" or less than a 5, what specific action can you take to improve?

_____

_____

_____

_____

_____

_____

LESSON #5:

The only way to create a life of liberty and fulfillment is through working with others. Leveraging others' efforts is a key aspect to scaling a business exponentially. You cannot be everything to everyone; you must empower your team!

Evaluate your current state of leveraging others' efforts.

There are tasks I am currently doing that others could be hired and trained to do.

Yes	No

(If Yes) What are those tasks, and when will you hire someone to do them?

_____

_____

_____

_____

_____

_____

_____

_____

_____

CHAPTER 3

THE GREAT ONES MOVE ON QUICKLY

After a few days, I drummed up the courage to reach out to Joe to let him know what had transpired. I took our portable phone out to my personal shed in the back yard and sat at the edge of my mattress, pondering what I might say. I turned on some of my favorite music to try to relax, because in my mind I was feeling like a failure. I looked around at the detached structure I called my bedroom, and felt pretty blessed to have such a cool room of my own apart from the house. It felt like my own apartment and gave me a sense of independence. I looked down at the phone in my hand and remembered why I had it there. It was time to face the facts and call Joe.

Joe answered quickly. I was secretly hoping it would go to his voicemail. "Hey Joe, it's Skylar. Can you talk?" I said.

"Skylar! Of course. How's my young entrepreneur friend?" he said fondly.

"Well, that's why I'm calling. We did pretty well in the snack-selling business, but then our school principal shut it down because he said we were competing with them. How was I supposed to know that? I felt like I was doing everything right and then bam, no more sweet-treat business!" I ranted.

Joe was silent for a moment. "Are you done complaining and feeling sorry for yourself now?" he said in a merciless tone.

I was caught off guard, thinking he was going to show a little more empathy, but I could sense another lesson coming, so I just said, "Yes, sir."

"Good, because you seemed to be going in a direction that is destructive, and that is not where champions live. Let me share another insight that is crucial for you to learn early in life, especially because there will be situations like this time and time again. Are you ready?" Joe asked.

I grabbed my notebook and gave Joe the green light to carry on with his lesson. He explained that in any set of circumstances, and especially the ones that are tough, I would have the choice to see the positive or the negative. Essentially, I could respond two different ways. The first is "Why me?" which fuels the victim and blame mentality, and leaves no room for improvement. The second option is definitely the higher road: "What can I learn?" This opens possibilities for improvement.

"So, Skylar, you now have a choice in this particular circumstance. Your snack business was shut down, but you must not let it shut you down. So, that being said, tell me something positive that came out of it," Joe insisted.

"Well, I guess through it all I made some decent money for a 15-year-old kid, hired a sales team to maximize my profits, and was able to help out my mom financially," I answered.

"And what did you learn by being shut down by your principal?" Joe asked.

After taking a moment to think about it, the realization came. "I need to make sure I do the proper research to make sure it is permissible to operate as a business. In this case, I probably should have asked the school administration if I was allowed to sell snacks on campus. Then I would have known in the beginning and could weigh the risk versus reward of operating the business."

Joe seemed satisfied with my answers and moved on quickly. "So what's next?"

"What do you mean, what's next?" I asked, a little confused.

"I mean, what business are you going to do next?" Joe repeated.

In a defeated tone I began, "Well, I think I am just going to do my job at Smart & Final and go to school. I am feeling a little burnt from this last business, and maybe it's just not the right . . ."

"Oh no, you don't. Great leaders don't live in 'poor me' thinking. There is absolutely no benefit to it. They get right back up after being knocked down, learn their lessons, and move on quickly. There is no time for a leader to curl up in the closet in the fetal position," Joe testified as if he were a preacher.

I didn't know how to respond, especially because no one had ever spoken to me that way before. Up to this point in my life, after providing an excuse as to why something did not work out, I was easily let off the hook. However, The CEO was speaking a whole new language to me. He had a higher expectation of me. There was no opportunity to be weak, there was no chance to give up, and I was really starting to recognize in a small measure why Joe was so successful. He was holding me accountable, and challenging my old mindsets and poor language.

Joe started in again. "Skylar, let me rephrase the question. What do you like to do and what are you good at?"

"I am good at a lot of things, I guess. I like music and car stereos and stuff. I also am intrigued with the internet and websites. I often think about designing different webpages," I answered.

"Well, there you go. A key element to finding fulfillment in any business is finding something you enjoy doing. How about you start a car stereo installation business among your high school friends, and start diving into designing people's websites?" Joe proposed.

"I think that I would really enjoy that!" I said.

"Awesome, Skylar! Go have fun with it."

With newfound energy, I recorded what Joe had said in my *CEO Lessons Learned* notebook.

LESSON #6: WHAT CAN I LEARN?

The difference between high achievers and people who end up quitting is how they view their life circumstances. What they ask themselves matters. "Why me?" fuels the victim and blame mentality and leaves no room for progression. The second option, "What can I learn?", is definitely the higher road and opens possibilities for progression and improvement.

LESSON #7: DO WHAT YOU ENJOY

A key element to finding fulfillment in any business is finding something you enjoy doing. Sometimes it can be the satisfaction of just running a quality business. And many times, it means hiring people to do the work you *don't* want to do.

I did as Joe suggested and started installing car stereos for my fellow high school students. I also created my own website design company, Prophecy Enterprises. I became fascinated with how the internet and marketing work in tandem. I used Flash software to build some pretty cool websites.

Over the next few years of high school, I often found myself skipping invitations to parties and other mindless activities to study marketing and how to create an effective business. When it was time to graduate high school, I decided I was going to become a realtor. I even opted out of my grad night parties to study for the real estate exam, so I could get started as soon as high school was over.

I passed the exam and felt launched into adult life. But then, almost a whole year passed, and I didn't sell a single house. I was very disappointed. I ended up calling Joe to see what his opinion was. I explained that no one wanted to buy a house from an 18-year-old kid, and that was why real estate was not working for me. His advice was not what I expected.

"That's an interesting statement, Skylar. Are you reading any books right now?" Joe inquired.

"Uh, I don't really like to read books unless I have to, and since I graduated high school, I'm not really required to read anymore," I admitted.

"Well, that just changed. The best leaders are the best readers, and your thinking about greater possibilities needs to expand. The fastest way to do that will be by reading books written by and about successful people, and learning their habits, success secrets, and proven processes. Somewhere along the line, you took on the belief that no one will buy a house from an 18-year-old kid, and congratulations, that's what you manifested!"

Joe had me write this quote down:

Joe continued to pour his priceless wisdom into me. "I want you to go to the bookstore this week and invest in these three books: *Think & Grow Rich*, by Napoleon Hill; *Rich Dad, Poor Dad*, by Robert Kiyosaki; and *Unleash the Power* Within, by Tony Robbins."

I must have sighed a little, because he continued, "Skylar, success leaves clues, and a major clue is that those who achieve greatly have a consistent habit of reading great books. Bill Gates reads 50 books a year. Warren Buffett attributes his accomplishments to reading 500 pages per day. Mark Cuban reads three hours a day. Tony Robbins says books saved his life from his alcoholic mother and several abusive fathers, and after taking a speed-reading course he read 700 books in 7 years. Elon Musk taught himself to build rockets by reading!"

I thanked Joe for the advice. I could see now how my weak thinking and low belief level created my lack of results as a realtor. I committed to investing in the books he recommended, and to reading consistently to increase my capacity to succeed. I also decided to move on quickly from real estate, as my heart was not in it anymore. I didn't anticipate the almost crippling road that lay ahead.

LESSON #8: READ

The best leaders are the best readers. Increase your knowledge and your thinking capacity through reading. Success leaves clues, and one major clue is that those who achieve greatly have a consistent habit of reading great books.

Review and Evaluations of Lessons Learned

LESSON #6:

The difference between high achievers and people who end up quitting is how they view their life circumstances. What they ask themselves matters. "Why me?" fuels the victim and blame mentality and leaves no room for progression. "What can I learn?" is the higher road and opens possibilities for progression and improvement.

In what area(s) of your life are you wondering, "Why me?" How can you switch to "What can I learn?"

_____

_____

_____

_____

_____

_____

_____

LESSON #7:

A key element to finding fulfillment in any business is finding something you enjoy doing. Sometimes it can be the fulfillment of just running a quality business. And many times, it means hiring people to do the work you *don't* want to do.

How much do you like what you do?
Circle your current, honest answer. 1 = Not at All and 5 = Always.

I regularly show up to my business with excitement.

1	2	3	4	5

If your answer is less than a 5, what specific action can you take to increase it to a level 5?

_____

_____

_____

_____

LESSON #8: THE BEST LEADERS ARE THE BEST READERS.

Increase your knowledge and your thinking capacity through reading. Success leaves clues, and one major clue is those who achieve greatly have a consistent habit of reading great books.

On average, how many books do you currently read a year? _____

Are you satisfied with your current reading habits?

Yes   No

If not, what are you going to do about it?

_____

_____

_____

_____

CHAPTER 4

LIFE HAPPENS FOR US, NOT TO US

I noticed my capacity and confidence increasing as I took time each day to read these great books. I found myself determined to start a business that would become very successful, and I was willing to do whatever it took to make it happen. I started searching for random businesses for sale and came across one that I knew for sure I could do. It was none other than an amazing hot dog stand. Even the name was brilliant: Big Dogz! The investment was only $8,000 to purchase the complete business, with supplies and all. The gentleman who sold it to me seemed like a nice guy and promised I would have the initial investment paid off within six months to a year. I was excited about the prospect of having a brick-and-mortar business of my own, so I plunged forward figuring out a way to buy it while naively trusting that the details would take care of themselves.

The truth is, at age 19 I did not have $8,000 to buy a business. Neither did anyone else I knew— besides Joe, of course, and I was not about to ask him for the money. I wanted to find a way to get my hot dog empire up and running on my own, and then impress Joe with my gold mine. I decided to get a few credit cards that I anticipated easily paying off as profits came in.

It was not long before Big Dogz was up and running and serving customers. Day after day, I did everything as a solo act: the cooking, serving, cleaning, purchasing, and accounting. In the beginning, I was super enthusiastic and had the energy to endure this much work, but soon I realized I had an issue. After I replenished my inventory, I was not making any profit. I was only making enough money to pay the minimum required amount on the credit cards I used to buy the business, and my other bills were not being met.

Over the course of several months, Joe called me a few times to check in, but I was too embarrassed to answer his calls, and found myself avoiding him. I applied for a few more credit cards to stay afloat, but after about a year I decided to close the doors (or rather the street corner) on Big Dogz, even though I was still heavily in debt. The man who sold me his hot dog stand made big promises that simply were not true, and I felt a bit jaded and defeated. Once again, it seemed like there was some invisible force making sure nothing worked out for me.

I reluctantly admitted that I should have called Joe for advice before I bought this turn-key wiener business with big promises—or at least answered his calls through the year. Owning up to my poor choices, I decided to call my CEO mentor to let him know what I had gotten myself into. I thought that he probably would not want to mentor me anymore—not the most productive thinking. But Joe picked up my call almost immediately with an enthusiastic tone. "Skylar! How have you been, champion? It's been way too long! I've tried calling you several times. Are you okay?"

"Hey Joe, I'm doing pretty good, and I'm sorry I didn't call you back. How are you?" I responded self-consciously.

"All is beautiful in my world, and no worries—I'm sure you had a good reason for it. What's going on with you? You don't sound so good."

I started to tell Joe about Big Dogz and how this dishonest man sold me his business, but before I could get too far, he cut me off.

"Did you research the important details, such as verifying the profit and loss statements, or did you test the market by surveying the customer base and locations before you purchased the hot dog stand?" Joe asked pointedly.

I paused for a moment, realizing my ignorance and lack of real business experience, and then responded, "No, I didn't think about that. I just trusted the guy and took his word for it. In the end, the man I bought it from got the victory and I got duped. How is this just? How is it that God lets people like this be successful?"

Joe patiently let me rant for a bit, then started in with a soft, mellow voice. "Skylar, God cares more about our character than our successes. God cares more about who we are, who we become, and how we represent Him. This dishonest man has his worldly reward, but it won't last long term. But here's my point: be sure to understand the numbers and market of any business you decide to get into!"

"But what am I supposed to do now? I have no income and a bunch of debt." If I sounded dejected, it's because I was.

"I am 100% confident you will figure that out, Skylar. There are some things I can't do for you, and honestly, I'm glad you had this experience because I know you'll never make the same mistake again. *Remember this:*

every experience, good or bad, serves as a mentor. Life happens for us, not to us. That's how high achievers always see it, so I trust you will see it that way, too," Joe concluded.

I thanked Joe for his mercy on me before we ended our phone call, and I promised to stay in touch more.

Over the next couple of years, I fell into a funk that I could not shake. I had moved out on my own, wanting to be independent of my mom, but now I couldn't afford my own apartment and I got evicted. I had to settle for a cheap room with a group of college guys in a townhouse.

My vision of being a CEO like Joe was starting to fade. I could not see the light at the end of the tunnel and attempted several odd jobs just to survive. I tried gambling for a time, delivering pizzas, being a loan officer, selling items on eBay, trading stocks, building websites, being a financial services agent, tile installation, manufactured home installation, and even a mobile spray-tanning booth. I didn't stick with any of them long-term.

My debts weighed heavy and just kept stacking up. I could see no way out. One of my roommates suggested I should just file for bankruptcy, and although I am not proud of it, I finally gave in. I found a local attorney that specialized in bankruptcy and made an appointment. I dreaded the day I had to essentially strip down financially in front of this attorney and list every single debt I had accumulated. It was flat-out humiliating, and the attorney's shocked reaction on how a person in their early twenties could have so much debt did not make the situation any better. I felt like I was giving up and not taking ownership of the situation I brought upon myself. I felt ashamed to talk about it with anyone, and sort of felt like a criminal when the attorney made sure I understood this would be on my personal record for a long time.

I was forced to literally sell all that I had, including my car. I fell into a trap of destructive behavior, going out partying multiple times a week. All I had was a measly mattress on the floor of a dingy room that was freezing because we decided not to turn on the heat to save money. It was the lowest point of my life, and although I had a room to stay in, I felt homeless with no possessions. The idea of reaching out to Joe had fled my mind, and I really did not know who to turn to.

One cold night I was in my rented bedroom, wondering how I could go on even one more day when I heard a faint knock at my door.

"Who is it?" I asked, without much interest.

"Skylar, are you in there?" A familiar voice came through the door.

"Dad, is that you?" Suddenly a wave of hope poured through me.

The door popped open and my dad peered through the doorway. Growing up, I had mainly lived with my mom. It was much easier living with her and my sister—my dad had remarried, and I had four other stepbrothers and sisters in his house. He had always been there for me, though. He glanced around at my poor circumstances, came directly over to me, and embraced me. I was a bit choked up inside but fought back the tears. My dad opened the box he brought in with him and revealed a little electric space heater. He went over and plugged it in.

"I just had a feeling to stop by and check on you, and I thought you might need this space heater for some reason. I guess I was right—it's freezing in here, son!" my dad said, shivering a bit.

"Thanks, Dad, this really means a lot to me. I have kind of hit a low point, and I feel like I've lost my sense of direction," I confessed. We talked about what I was going through for a while before Dad brought it back to something he'd told me many times before.

"I understand, son, but you know I've learned that everything always works out in the end. *If it hasn't worked out, it's not the end,*" Dad said, smiling as he repeated his mantra.

It was a short visit, but it was exactly what I needed. A fog seemed to lift, and even though my circumstances were pitiful, a sense of peace began to settle in. I found myself expressing a simple prayer of gratitude for my father's inspiration to bring me an electric space heater. I also pleaded for help, which I had not done in a long time because I felt so unworthy. I recalled and seemed to relate to the account of the prodigal son in the New Testament—how his father rejoiced for his return even after all his riotous living. My father and I enjoyed a stronger bond after that night. His simple act of kindness and love provided a much-needed emotional boost.

Once my dad left, my mind turned to my other mentor, The CEO. It had been a couple of years since our last talk, but now that Dad had given me some hope, I started thinking about what Joe had been teaching me. I took out my notebook and looked at my notes from our last talk.

LESSON #9: CHARACTER COUNTS

Care more about your character than your success.

LESSON #10: KNOW YOUR NUMBERS

Understand your business numbers, especially when buying a business. Many people fail in business due to lack of attention to their numbers.

I slept warm that night, and I feel like it helped me think straight, because I woke up determined to make something happen. I gained the confidence to call Joe, and although he was not available, his voice message recording was just what I needed to hear. His familiar, warm voice said, *"Remember, life does not determine a champion: a champion determines life!"*

That simple recorded message was another lesson learned, and I was about to note it down when Joe called me back.

"Hey, Skylar, I see you called. How are things going?" Joe asked. Two years later, and he calls back and sounds like we'd talked yesterday!

"Doing better now—thanks for asking. But you know, Joe, I'm just not where I want to be. I've never been so low in my life, and I figured I would be so much more successful by this point in my life." I proceeded to tell Joe all the dirty details of what I had experienced.

"Hmm. At age 22, I would say you are exactly where you are supposed to be," Joe responded. "In fact, even if you were 41, you would be exactly where you are supposed to be."

"I don't understand. How can this be exactly where I am supposed to be when so many things have gone wrong?" I argued.

Joe paused a moment before he taught me my next valuable lesson. "Skylar, consider for a moment everything that has gone *right* for you. What I mean is, all these experiences you are having are qualifying you for greater opportunities. No one just gets success handed to them. You can't get to the top by simply taking the elevator—you must take the stairs, and sometimes there are a lot of floors to climb. Many people are not willing to take the stairs because they see the elevator as an option." I had to admit that had a familiar ring.

"My point is," Joe continued, "these times you are experiencing are not hard times at all. They are character-shaping times, refining times, and they qualify you for greater heights. So, like I said, you are exactly where you are supposed to be. Your victories will taste so much sweeter because you have drunk of the bitter times. You'll experience the simple day-to-day luxuries in life with so much more gratitude from now on, because they have been stripped from you."

"I guess I can see your point, Joe. In the thick of it all, and with so many more floors to climb, I've considered quitting," I admitted.

"Everybody has moments like that. Do you know what the opposite of success is, Skylar?" Joe asked.

Figuring I had the right answer, I confidently said, "Failure, right?"

"Nope. The opposite of success is giving up. The *only* way you fail is if you quit. So you hold the key to whether you shut your doors on success. No one else," Joe stated.

"I understand now, Joe. Thank you for setting me straight," I said humbly.

"Here's the last thing I will tell you, and then I need to run. There are so many great opportunities in your future, and many key strategies and systems that I am going to show you that will help you become a two-day a week CEO. However, most of this learning is above the 20th floor, and you are still climbing the first few stories. Hang in there and keep going, never give up. Write this down. Look up Romans 8:28 in the New Testament. That will validate everything I just shared with you," Joe said as he bid me farewell for now.

After we hung up, I looked up Romans 8:28. It reads, "And we know that in all things God works for the good of those who love him, who have been called according to his purpose."

Joe's straight talk helped me come to see that my weak mindset and lack of discipline had created my current set of circumstances, and unless I snapped out of it, things would keep going downhill. I didn't have all the answers, but I knew that things were going to get better somehow. According to The CEO and the Book of Romans, apparently all these challenges were opportunities for my growth, and in some way, happening for my good. Little did I know things were about to get better—a lot better— and it would be largely because of a beautiful girl.

REVIEW AND EVALUATIONS OF LESSONS LEARNED

LESSON #9:

Care more about your character than your success.

Circle your current honest answer. 1 = Not at All and 5 = Absolutely

I am personally true to my character and honest in all my dealings.

1   2   3   4   5

I am willing to fire my best team member if their character doesn't align with our company values.

1   2   3   4   5

If your answers are less than a 5, what specific actions can you take to increase to a level 5?

_____

_____

_____

_____

LESSON #10:

Understand your business numbers, especially when buying a business. Many people fail in business due to a lack of attention to their numbers.

Circle your current honest answer.
1 = Not at All and 5 = Absolutely

I understand my profit and loss and balance sheet numbers very well.

| 1 | 2 | 3 | 4 | 5 |

I regularly review my business numbers.

| 1 | 2 | 3 | 4 | 5 |

If your answers are less than a 5,
what specific actions can you take to increase to a level 5?

_____

_____

_____

_____

CHAPTER 5

THE TURNING POINT

My thoughts and behavior towards girls were a bit tainted through my adolescent years. I can admit that at times, before I knew any better, a girl was nothing more to me than an object to satisfy my own pleasure. Many times I let skanky material and images creep into my life. Coming from a family with divorced parents, I often wondered what true love really looked like, so you could say I was a novice when it came to relationships.

One of the random jobs I took on to stay afloat after my bankruptcy was a bathroom attendant at a popular dance club. At first it felt a bit shameful to be the guy to give men their hand towel and ask if they wanted any breath mints after they used the restroom. However, after a few nights of making $300 in tips, I didn't care what other people thought. It was a mindless job, and the environment and music seemed to ease my senses.

Occasionally, when I was not on the clock as a bathroom attendant, I would go to the dance club as a patron. It allowed me to let loose a bit, and there were a lot of pretty girls that showed up. One particular night, my mind was focused on only one girl in the whole dance club: Jessica. Something was different with her, and I found myself wanting to raise my game as a person just by being close to her. I knew exactly who she was, although I was not sure she remembered who I was. A short time before seeing her at the club, I had been hired on with a financial services company, and she was the superstar of that whole organization. There were hundreds of agents, and I was at the lowest level for over two years with no promotions before I ended up quitting.

I began to move in closer, so she knew I was in her dance zone. I would occasionally get close and make brief contact, then I would back off a bit to see if she noticed me. We ended up dancing all night and into the early morning, and from my point of view, we were dialed into each other. She was beautiful inside and out, and our chemistry on the dance floor was creating something that kept us close to each other the whole time. Then came the moment of truth. The last song was being played, so I decided to test the waters by doing the good old "take away method." Before the last song was over, I began to make my way to the exit without saying anything. I am not sure what I was thinking, but it worked beautifully because Jessica grabbed me from behind, demanding that I not leave without saying goodbye. It worked, and she gave me her number!

That night I was on a love high, but the fact was that I had absolutely nothing when it came to material possessions. Jessica, on the other hand, was already extremely successful at age 23, with her own condo, a 5-Series BMW, and a great lifestyle. I knew I wanted to call her to further the relationship but was terrified of her discovering my lowly circumstances. I knew I needed some sound advice, so the next day I decided to call Joe.

I explained to Joe how Jessica and I came together like magnets on the dance floor, and how I did the old takeaway move at the end. He let out a hearty laugh and then got down to business.

"So, what's your next move, Skylar? You have her phone number, right?" Joe probed.

"Yeah. I do have her phone number, and I want to ask her out on a date, but if she finds out about my impoverished, undisciplined life, there is no way she'll want anything to do with me!" I explained in a hopeless tone of voice.

"Is that how you see yourself, Skylar—impoverished and undisciplined?" Joe asked.

I took a moment to evaluate my response, recognizing there was more to his question. "I don't *want* to see myself that way, but I can't get past the stains from my past. For a moment, dancing with her felt amazing, and I was able to forget my past and imagine something new."

"And what did that something new look like?" Joe continued.

"I saw my life with her. I saw me rising up to something greater than a life that has plagued me in the past. I wanted to do whatever it takes to be worthy of her," I admitted.

"It sounds like you found a true gem, then. That's exactly what the right woman should do for you. So, what are you scared of?" Joe inquired.

"I think I'm scared of rejection. She's probably way out of my league," I confessed.

"She is way out of your league, Skylar, from what I am understanding about her. But when did anyone get better at anything by playing in leagues below their level? If you want to step up to the next level, you must play up, rise up, and man up!" Joe said, with some power in his voice.

The CEO shared a valuable lesson with me that applied to both my desired relationship with Jessica and business. He said that *if my fears outweighed my desired result or goal, the fears would dominate, and nothing would get accomplished. On the flip side, if my goal outweighed my fear, I would find the courage to move forward to make it happen.* Focus on what you want to happen, not on what you don't want to happen.

"So, what's your goal or desired result, Skylar?" The CEO questioned.

"I want to go on a date with Jessica and further our relationship," I stated confidently.

"Are you going to let your fear of rejection or the fear that she is out of your league paralyze you into not calling her?" Joe asked.

"Of course not, I'm going to call her as soon as we hang up!" I declared.

"That's more like it. Keep me posted, champion." I could hear Joe's smile over the phone.

Just after Joe and I hung up, he texted me a powerful quote to give me an extra boost.

> "Our doubts are traitors, and make us lose the good we often might win, by fearing to attempt."
> **–Ralph Waldo Emerson**

Now I was determined to call Jessica to set up a date, even though I had no car and very little money to my name. The phone call to Jessica was easier than I made it out to be, and we agreed on a lunch date the following week.

Fortunately, my dad let me borrow his work Astro Van for the next few months. Unfortunately, it smelled terrible and moldy because of his carpet-cleaning equipment in the back. The van was old and clunky, and there was no way I was going to pull up in front of the restaurant in that thing, so I parked a few blocks away to conceal it. We met at an American-Asian cafe, and I wore a baggy brown suit—it was the best I had at the time. I guess I felt a suit would make me look more professional even though I didn't have a real job or business.

Our first date was amazing, and before we knew it, we were inseparable. Our goals and vision for life aligned perfectly. Crazily enough, Jessica was living in the exact same condo complex I was living in. The difference was, she owned her condo and had furniture—and I was just renting a nearly naked room.

It was not long before we were discussing plans to take our relationship to another level, and I knew I had to do something other than just a job if I wanted to rise to Jessica's expectations. It was time for me to start a business that would last. It was sort of a do-or-die moment. This was going to work, or I was going to have to hang up any aspirations of having my own company and being a CEO like Joe.

It was 2009 and the housing market was in a downward frenzy. Many people's equity in their homes was dropping 30-50% after a long period of inflated home prices, and almost overnight, many owed much more on their house than what it was worth.   The banks who held the mortgage notes were willing to renegotiate the loan to accommodate for the correction in the market. It was a tedious process with a mountain of paperwork, and people were willing to pay money up front to get the process done. A friend of mine started a business helping people figure out how to save their home through a loan modification. There was obviously a demand, but he didn't know how to market effectively to get a steady stream of customers. I felt like I did, so I decided to pursue the opportunity on my own.

I sought out a reputable mortgage company that specialized in the loan modification process and told them I could be their marketing and sales division and bring them deals. They agreed to pay me 25% of the $3000 processing fee clients paid, which meant a $750 profit for every client I brought to the table who made a deal. I was excited about the prospect of it all, but there was one hurdle. How would I get the people?

I searched out a direct mailing company that could pinpoint certain demographics and zip codes. I designed an advertisement to entice people to pursue a loan modification with a phone number to call. Each mailer piece was one dollar, and the company required a minimum of one thousand mailers to start. I had everything lined up to launch my marketing company—except for the $1000, of course.

Obviously, Jessica had the money. But we had only been dating two months and I was hesitant to jeopardize our relationship.

As I contemplated what to do, I recalled my last conversation with The CEO. My goals and vision to be successful with this opportunity were way too big to let fear stop me. With one thousand mailers going out, I only needed to sell one client on a loan modification, and I would make back almost my entire initial investment. Nonetheless, I called Joe again to seek his advice.

"Wow, Skylar, great job on all the research and lining up all of the necessary players to make this happen!" Joe congratulated me after I explained all the business details.

"Thanks, Joe, but do you think I should move forward on it?" I was looking for more validation.

"Skylar, listen close. Great leaders know how to make big decisions without hesitation after they do their research. They avoid indecision because that's the worst decision. Many people never get what they want in life because they never decide what that is and take action! I love what Ralph Waldo Emerson said on the matter: *'When a decision is made, the universe conspires to make it happen.'* So go on and decide! Move forward or forget the whole thing, but either way, make a decision," Joe concluded.

Joe's counsel was just what I needed to hear, and I wrote it down as another lesson learned. I took confidence in the fact that I had really searched this out and had all the pieces lined up. The idea of not pursuing this opportunity would only leave me in my current set of pitiful financial circumstances. This was a chance to do something big, and I was not about to let a measly thousand dollars keep me from it.

While riding as a passenger with Jessica in her 5-series BMW, I walked her through my big idea. Then I popped the question—asking for a one-thousand-dollar loan. At first, she said she promised herself that she would never loan a boyfriend money and would never stay with someone who asked her for money. Somehow, I overcame those two objections, because she agreed to loan me the money. I caught her at an interesting time in her life, as she had recently transitioned out of financial services and was looking for a new challenge. She not only lent me the money; she got on board with helping run the company!

The mailers were sent out, and then it was a waiting game. With each passing day and no phone calls, that negative force kept attacking my thoughts. *"What if no one calls?" "See? You are going to fail again!"* I found myself praying and walking a lot. I always made sure my cell phone was charged, waiting for that first call.

Shortly thereafter, I was walking outside of a coffee shop in Temecula, CA, when my phone rang with an unknown number. Hoping it was a potential customer, I answered as if I were in a professional office. It was indeed, and I closed my first deal for $3000 on the spot. I was so excited to tell Jessica that it worked! Over the next few days, a couple more calls came in and I closed two more deals!

We had now made some decent profit from sending out one thousand direct-mail pieces. I asked Joe what we should do next, and he wisely asked me, "Where did those deals come from in the first place?" Of course—it was from the direct mailers. So, he told us to put all of our earned money back into the company by sending out more mailers. He also reiterated that oftentimes in the beginning of a business, the leaders must be willing to forgo a salary to make sure the company launches.

I took Joe's advice and put all the profit back into more mailers, which proved to be an amazing decision. We did this over and over for the next six weeks. My life was beginning to turn out like I wanted. Major success was about to show up in my life—along with some of my old behaviors.

LESSON #11: DECIDE

Great leaders know how to make big decisions without hesitation after they do the research. They avoid indecision because that is the worst decision. Many people never get what they want in life because they never decide what that is and take action!

REVIEW AND EVALUATIONS OF LESSONS LEARNED

LESSON #11:

Great leaders know how to make big decisions without hesitation after they do the research. They avoid indecision because that is the worst decision.

Evaluate your current level of making decisions personally and in your capacity as a leader. Circle your current, honest answer. 1 = Very Hesitant and 5 = Confidently

I make personal decisions swiftly and effectively.

1   2   3   4   5

I make business decisions swiftly and effectively.

1   2   3   4   5

If your answers are less than a 5,
what specific actions can you take to increase them to a level 5?

_____

_____

CHAPTER 6

WE ALL MAKE MISTAKES

After a short period of time, Jessica and I were closing dozens of loan-modification deals, and our sights were set on many more. I rewarded myself by purchasing a modest car and set up an official company called Lewis Marketing. We were ready to take both the company and our relationship to the next level.

My mind was a little disoriented by the glory of business success and having an incredible girl whom I honestly did not feel worthy of. I was a little scared about the whole situation, and I am not proud to say that I let my own insecurities drive me to do the dumbest thing in my life up to that point. In my messed-up thinking, I figured Jessica would not want to be with me long term anyway, so somehow, I found a way to try and make that a reality. I sabotaged myself.

By now, Jessica and I had been together several months, and we had committed to be exclusive to one another. My upbringing didn't provide me with what an ideal relationship looked like, or how to be exclusive to any one person. I frankly lacked commitment and maturity. One night, I made one of the worst decisions of my life and cheated on the woman I finally felt was meant for me.

The moment after it happened, I was devastated by my selfish, lustful decision. I became terribly sick to my stomach with guilt and was overcome with the feeling that there was no hope for me anymore. I got in my car and argued out loud with myself mercilessly. *How could you let a moment's pleasure ruin something so potentially long-lasting and special?* In my despair I drove straight to Joe's Southern California house, hoping he would be there. I desperately needed to talk to someone.

As I drove up to his house, I noticed the lights were on, and through the large front window I could see Joe and his family sitting at the dinner table, happily enjoying each other's company. His boys, Joey and Jeremy, were older now and looked like miniature versions of Joe. My eyes welled up with tears as I wondered if I would ever have a family like his. I did not want to disrupt their family dinner, but I also knew I needed to talk with him. Joe's advice of letting my goal outweigh my fear served me well in that very moment, and I apprehensively approached his door.

I attempted to gain my composure before I rang the doorbell, but my emotions were raw, and tears just kept coming. Joe turned on the porch light and peered through the front door peep hole to see who it was. I am sure I looked pretty bad, but nonetheless the door was immediately opened.

"Skylar, are you okay? What happened?" Joe said anxiously.

His simple question caused me to crumble emotionally and I began to sob. Joe approached me and wrapped me in his arms, not knowing what I was dealing with but seeing that I was yearning for some comfort.

"Come in and sit down, Skylar. Tell me what's going on," Joe said as he led me into his front room.

Fighting back the tears, I began. "I really messed up this time, Joe, and I don't know why I did it. Why do I keep making things worse once they are so good?"

Joe handed me a box of tissues and asked for clarification. "What do you mean, Skylar? What did you do that you feel you messed up?"

"I cheated on Jessica tonight. She's the only girl I've ever felt I wanted to be with forever, and I threw all of that away and cheated on her," I admitted. The confession caused me to sob uncontrollably and bury my face in my hands.

Joe sat patiently and quietly, letting me cry out my feelings.

"I mean what was I *thinking* to do something so stupid? Jessica will never want to be with me again! On top of that, our new business is going so good, and we work so well together. And I threw it all away!"

Finally, Joe responded, "Oh, I don't know about that, Skylar. It doesn't make sense to try and think for other people or determine how they will respond to a situation. That's a hundred percent their choice, not yours. If she decides she's done with you, then so be it, but she may also forgive you if you show her you are truly sorry and promise to stay true from now on. You'll have to rebuild her trust in you. The fact that you are so sorrowful about this shows you really care about Jessica. Something has changed in you to want to leave your old careless lifestyle for a more virtuous and responsible one."

Joe's compassionate perspective had never crossed my mind and offered a small measure of peace and hope. It also allowed me to gather my emotions.

He continued, "When you are ready, you must ask Jessica for forgiveness and beg her to give you another chance."

"Thank you for listening to me, and for all your generous help over the years. I'm sure I don't deserve it most of the time," I said.

"Listen here, Skylar, that sorry attitude needs to shift right now," Joe said with some heat. "You do deserve it, and you are worthy of my time and energy or I would not have agreed to be your mentor in the beginning. Though you may be tempted to give up on yourself, I will never quit on you. We all make mistakes—all of us. We were not sent to this earth to walk through life perfectly without any pitfalls. Focus on what you can do and let go of the things that are out of your control," Joe counseled.

I left Joe's house gratefully in control of my emotions and thoughts. He had a gifted way to help me see the forest from the trees. I was determined to tell Jessica eventually what I had done and beg for her forgiveness.

Our days continued to be filled with more and more sales calls, and we closed several more deals weekly. I stayed focused moving our business forward, although painful flashes of guilt of my self-sabotaging actions surfaced in my mind often. I knew I was going to confess to Jessica; I just was not sure when. I remembered Joe's comforting words on the night I made that terrible mistake happen and jotted them down in my *Lessons Learned* notebook.

LESSON #12: MISTAKES

We all make mistakes. We were not sent to this earth to walk through life perfectly without any pitfalls. Focus on what you can do and let go of the things that are out of your control.

Within a month of launching the Lewis Marketing Corporation, Jessica expressed how she had always wanted to live in the San Diego area and suggested that we move both our personal lives and our business from her condo in Murrieta, California (which was our current business headquarters). At this point, her wish was my command, so we found a good deal on some office space in Carlsbad just north of San Diego and made plans to move our operation.

While packing up our belongings (mostly Jessica's belongings), she came across my *Lessons Learned* notebook and wondered what it was. Before I could explain or attempt to get it back from her, she opened its pages and began to browse through what I had written. She paused and read the last one I had written. It must have struck an emotional chord because her eyes filled up with tears as she looked up at me while tenderly pressing the notebook against her chest.

"What is this, Skylar, and who is The CEO?" Jessica inquired as she wiped her eyes.

I took Jessica's hand and sat her down on the couch to explain. "I was going to tell you about him when it was the right time, and now seems to be like that time. The CEO is my mentor, and he has been helping me since I was 15 years old. His name is Joe. The summer before my sophomore year, some buddies of mine and I thought it would be thrilling to sneak into a restaurant he owns. A cop noticed us inside, and my buddies escaped ahead of me, and I ended up getting arrested. The police officer called Joe and he rushed over. Joe had mercy on me, took me to his house, and we made a deal that if I came and worked at his restaurant as community service the rest of the summer, he wouldn't press charges."

"So, you broke into some successful guy's business and now he's your mentor?" she asked sarcastically.

"Well, yes! From the moment I met Joe, I wanted to be like him. He has a beautiful wife, two amazing boys, and is the CEO of a couple of multi-million-dollar companies. The phenomenal thing about it is he has figured out how to successfully run his companies while being at his office less than two days a week."

"Wow, seriously? That's impressive. I've never seen any business owner accomplish that long-term." Jessica raised her eyebrows.

"Exactly. I did everything he asked me to do and began noting down in this notebook my lessons learned every time he gave me advice. Joe was impressed with me wanting to diligently learn from him and achieve some of the things he had, so he offered to mentor me. My lessons have been about both life and business," I finished.

Jessica started reading from the beginning and was enthralled with all of my lessons learned from The CEO. I just sat and watched her take them all in.

"Okay, I'm ready to meet him. Especially before we move to San Diego. Can you set up a meeting with him?" Jessica asked enthusiastically, ready to take immediate action.

"There's nothing I'd like better," I responded.

Joe agreed to meet Jessica and I at his southern California house the next day. Jessica had been well trained to learn from experienced mentors and coaches throughout her career, and knew the immense value of it.

Joe greeted us both with a hug and invited us to come in and sit down in his front room. However, Jessica gravitated to Joe's family pictures on the wall and curiously asked about them.

While she was a safe distance away from Joe and I, he leaned in and whispered, "She is a beautiful girl, Skylar, and I can tell there is definitely something special about her."

I quickly responded back in a similar hushed tone, "Thank you, I agree."

Then Joe turned his focus back to Jessica, who was still browsing the family pictures, and told us where the pictures were taken and how he met Karen, his wife. I learned a simple, valuable lesson from Jessica that day.

We explained our plans to scale our business in the San Diego area, and we also shared the success we were having with just the two of us. We both knew we would need to hire more people, but wanted to get Joe's advice on our process. Upon our asking, The CEO stood up from his seat and asked to be excused for a moment. He went into his home office and brought back a large spiral-bound book. I caught a glimpse of the title on the front cover: *The 2-Day-CEO Leadership Guide Book.*

I glanced over at Jessica for a moment, and I am sure we were thinking the exact same thing: *How do we get a copy of that book?*

Oblivious to our desires, Joe looked at the table of contents and easily found the section he was looking for. "Aha, here it is! If you want to scale your call center, here is the most effective way to do it. Actually, I'll just make a copy of this section for each of you so you can have it."

Our eyes grew wide, and before I knew it Jessica was elbowing me in my side. I knew what she was implying, so I asked. "Joe, thanks so much for being willing to copy that section for us. Can we get a copy of that whole book?"

"Not yet Skylar, not yet. You are not ready for the whole thing. There is too much to digest right now, so I will share with you the sections that are most pertinent as we check in with each other more frequently. But I like your forward thinking!" Joe said as he whistled his way to his copy machine.

Joe returned after a brief moment and handed us each a copy of the section that was entitled *Simplify to Scale*. "Study this section carefully and follow what it says. Then check in with me and we'll talk about other sections as they're needed," he instructed.

We both expressed our sincere gratitude to The CEO and promised to be in touch. Then we made our way towards our new home base in Carlsbad, California.

REVIEW AND EVALUATIONS OF LESSONS LEARNED

LESSON #12: WE ALL MAKE MISTAKES.

We were not sent to this earth to walk through life perfectly without any pitfalls. Focus on what you can do, and let go of the things that are out of your control.

In what area(s) of your life and business do you need to surrender and release control?

_____

_____

_____

_____

SIMPLIFY TO SCALE

With Jessica in the passenger seat, we wasted no time and she began to read the excerpt *Simplify to Scale* section in the "The Systems" chapter from The CEO's leadership guidebook. I listened intently as I drove.

> "Any fool can complicate things. It takes a genius to simplify."
> – Albert Einstein

McDonalds uses the philosophy "Keep It Simple." They can take 21-year-old high-school graduates and have them run an entire restaurant—a multi-million-dollar restaurant! Can a 21-year-old run your entire business? Can an experienced adult run your entire business?

The answer is, "Probably not—yet." The business is most likely too complex and lacking proper systemization. You must learn to simplify

99

your business and build processes that are duplicatable. Duplication is key. The quickest way to grow a company is to simplify a process and then duplicate it over and over. *First simplify, then duplicate.*

A couple years ago, I brought on a very experienced, high-level executive to our team. He knew our industry well. One of the first things he said to me was, "I've never seen this before. You have regular people who have minimal industry experience performing better than some of the more experienced people I have worked with. Your system has made it easy to take regular performers and make them great." His model was to hire the most experienced person he could possibly find. That was all he knew. I have come to learn something different. I knew that we could take an inexperienced person who had a great attitude and was a good culture fit, plug them into our system, and they would perform at a high level.

Even though the executive understood this, he still could not wrap his mind around building a simple process for people to follow. He would go on sales calls with new trainees, and I would ask the trainee how it went. They would say, "Wow, he really knows his stuff. He was amazing and talked about all his experience, knowledge, and so on to the customer." Then I would ask if they could do that same presentation. They would look at me hesitantly and say, "Not like that." The exec didn't follow a script or do it the same way each time. So, everyone that trained with him was left feeling unconfident and unsure that they could ever sell like he did. They thought they needed 20 years of experience.

Are you getting it? Whenever you are building anything within your company, ask this very important question: Is it duplicatable? Can someone else do it the same exact way?

What makes something duplicatable?

Simplicity.

Start looking at the sales process within your company. If you are the owner and you are still selling, start to identify how you can simplify your sales process. If you are doing a sales presentation or sales call, don't wing it and throw in anything needed to get the sale done. Break down the things you say and write them down. Script it. Figure out how you can delete anything that another salesperson might not be able to say.

Example: If you talk about how you are the owner and you will work directly with the customer, your sales person will never be able to say that. You need to remove that from your presentation. If you want to get out of selling at your company, simplify the process so others can do it.

If you are working on a process within your company, think about how to simplify that process so it can be duplicatable. How many steps are in that process? Write them out. You would be surprised at the number of things that need to be done in one process.

Example: Take call from customer, enter the information into the contact management software, make sure to verify the address, schedule a second call with the customer, confirm with the sales rep who will be handling the customer, verify their availability, etc.

What is *not* duplicatable?

Let's start with what is challenging to duplicate: intuition.

As a leader, you will typically have better intuition than your team members about the facets of your business. If you are training your manager how to properly hire people, you won't be able to share your intuition with them, because that is gained from years of experience in making good and bad decisions. It also comes from experiences that have happened "to" you. Intuition is unique to each individual. If you hire people based on a feeling or your gut, that is not duplicatable. It must be quantifiable.

How do you systemize something like this? Have the candidate take a personality profile. If that personality matches the position, a box is checked. If the applicant answers a pre-set series of questions correctly, another box is checked. If you want your team to be effective at hiring or any process that involves intuition, get it out of your head and onto paper so they can duplicate it.

Another factor impossible to duplicate is experience.

Your experience in managing jobs, people, customers, etc. is very hard to duplicate. Let's say you are in the construction industry and you have a very skilled project manager that you want to have train a new team member. You must get that project manager to share how he makes decisions. If he decides to use a certain type of lumber versus another one, he probably gained that insight from past experiences. Get that on paper. Get everything documented so you can duplicate what that project manager does and how he thinks about things.

Any time your experience or intuition is necessary for a process in your company to be successful, replace it with a documented process that can be duplicated. Strive to simplify and remove these additional complexities. Take the experience out of someone's head and document it.

You will know if you have duplication/simplification issues if you continue to hire team members who are not able to do the work properly. If you see a new team member who doesn't understand how to do their role or is very challenged by it, it may be a sign that you need to simplify their role and process. You may just have the wrong team member—but chances are, you can definitely make their job easier.

I am always focused on simplifying. I am always asking our team, "How do we make this simpler? What can we cut out? What part of this process is not needed?"

A great way to start this process is to start documenting your procedures. In the business world, those are called Standard Operating Procedures, or SOPs. Documenting your procedures eliminates the guesswork and creates a systemized approach. SOPs will be discussed more in Chapter 15.

After Jessica read through the *Simplify to Scale* section, she took the liberty of noting down the lesson learned in what had just become our mutual CEO Notebook.

LESSON #13: SIMPLIFY TO SCALE

Simplicity and uniform processes create scalable duplication. Constantly identify what can be cut out to make things simpler. SOPs eliminate the guesswork and create an effective systemized business. Document all of your most important processes.

We immediately acted and began to script our sales calls from the initial greeting all the way to the close of the deal. That way, anyone with basic sales and people skills could take calls and close deals. We did not want to leave anything to chance when it came to the call process. We scripted how to handle objections in order to move prospects from their insecurities to comfortably moving forward. We also documented how we wanted our SOPs to look for a sales rep and a future manager.

After following the CEO's guidelines, we felt confident that we could plug people into our system and get great results. I reached out to a friend of mine, Adam, who I knew was a good salesman and would pick up our process quickly. He agreed to come onboard, and we spent a full day role-playing the scripts and objections with him. He proved very helpful in handling our call volume for the loan modifications.

We grew exponentially in a short amount of time and hired two more sales reps nearly every month. We constantly tested new advertising hooks on our mailers until we found the one that produced the best results. Then we doubled down on the winner with our marketing budget. It was amazing! Within 12 months, we were investing over $40,000 a month in mailers to keep the leads flowing in. We had over 20 sales reps and had appointed a manager to handle the operations. Jessica and I started coming in three to four days a week and were beginning to taste what it was like to be a 2-Day-CEO.

I still had a lot to learn, though. One day, my friend Adam, whom we hired in the very beginning, approached me and wanted to talk. He seemed upset.

"Hey, Adam, what's up?" I asked as he took a seat in my office.

"So, I see you and Jessica hardly coming into the office anymore," Adam started.

"Yeah, is there a problem?" I inquired.

"I'm here every day, Monday through Saturday, busting my tail to get more deals while you and Jessica stroll in and reap all of the profits!" Adam vented in a heated tone.

"Hold on there, buddy, chill out. We pay you very well for every deal you close, and frankly, a lot more than the other sales reps. What is this really about, Adam?" I fired back.

"I don't know. I guess I feel like a peasant working for his master. I see how many deals we are closing every day, and I know we are already well over a million dollars in sales. I know I didn't start this company, but why should you be making so much more than me?" Adam continued.

I didn't know how to console my friend and was confused with the whole situation. We continued to argue, and eventually Adam walked out of my office and never returned. We have never spoken again since that day. I felt like I should have been able to handle the situation with Adam, but I obviously needed to learn something. I wasted no time in reaching out to Joe.

Joe was pleased and excited to hear we had scaled our business so quickly by duplicating our processes effectively. After I explained what had happened with Adam, he taught me a valuable lesson. He said, "While it is certainly okay to hire friends and even family as team members, if the proper expectations are not set in the beginning for their specific role and your role in the company as the leader, resentment may be the result. They see you as their equal because they know you personally. Resentment and hurt feelings can be avoided by simply establishing agreed-upon expectations in the beginning."

I chalked it up as another lesson learned–the hard way.

LESSON #14: HOW TO HIRE FRIENDS

It's okay to hire friends and family as team members if the proper expectations are set in the beginning for their specific role and your role in the company as the leader. If they are not, resentment and hurt feelings may result.

We continued to plug away in our business, and I was humbled that at age 23, we had our first million-dollar business. Jessica and I started to talk about our future plans for the business, and more importantly, for us as a couple. She was the only one I wanted to be with for the rest of my life, and I had plans to make that more concrete.

REVIEW AND EVALUATIONS OF LESSONS LEARNED

Lesson #13: Simplicity and uniform processes create scalable duplication. Constantly identify what can be cut out to make things simpler. Standard Operating Procedures eliminate the guesswork and create an effective systemized business. Document all of your important processes.

Evaluate your current level of simplifying to scale.
Circle your current, honest answer. 1 = Not at All and 5 = Absolutely

We have uniform processes that are followed by our team.

1	2	3	4	5

We have SOPs in place for each major process in the company.

1	2	3	4	5

Our SOPs are known and clear in our company.

1	2	3	4	5

Our company processes are simple and duplicatable.

1   2   3   4   5

If any of your answers are less than a 5,
what specific actions can you take to increase them to a level 5?

_____

_____

_____

_____

CHAPTER 8

HERE WE GROW AGAIN

It was December, and Lewis Marketing was going strong. We had over 20 trained sales reps and a manager who was running the daily operations. I felt like Jessica and I needed a little vacation from it all. For the most part, we were now comfortable leaving the business to run without us for at least a week or two, so I put together a little surprise for Jessica. Actually, it was not little at all. It was a huge surprise.

I wanted to take her somewhere extraordinary, classy, a place known for romance. With our business and profits doing so well, I could dream a little bigger, so I booked a romantic trip to Paris, France. It might have seemed like an extremely elaborate trip to take after being exclusively together for such a short period. However, this was not going to be just any trip. This would be the trip in which I proposed marriage to the love of my life.

We flew to Europe that next month. We strolled through Paris holding hands like two young love birds. It was surreal to be in a place we had only seen in pictures. When the sun set, the city lights peeked through the misty air, and we felt like we were in a romantic movie. Our five-star hotel was divine and worth the investment. We dined like a king and queen.

The night arrived for me to carry out my strategically planned proposal. We had discussed marriage on occasion and what that might look like, but as far as I knew, Jessica was not expecting me to move forward on it yet. That day, we planned to see some of the major sites, such as the Eiffel Tower, and finish off the evening at the Louvre Museum.

While at the world-renowned Louvre, we walked around the outside holding hands and talking about our future. The sky at dusk presented us with the most brilliant blue we had ever seen, and we were swallowed up in the magic of it all. The moment was perfect. I felt the heavens were smiling down on us and on my decision to make this beautiful and kind-hearted woman my wife. I easily imagined her as an amazing mother to our future children, and someone I would be excited to come home to every day for the rest of my life.

I began to breathe a little heavier as my nerves recognized what I was about to do. To distract her a little, I suggested she get a panoramic video of the entire Louvre and its surrounding courtyard and handed her my video camera. I gazed at her slowly circling around taking it all in. When she returned full circle back to me, I was on one knee with the ring in my hand. She unexpectedly blurted out a scream with her hands pressed against her lips. She—and everyone else around us—knew what was coming next.

I expressed how much she meant to me, how she was the only one I wanted to be with for the rest of my life, and how much I loved her. Then, of course, I popped the question. Tears filled both of our eyes as she reached out for my embrace and said, "Yes!" We just held each other for a while and may have kissed a time or two–in Paris! at the Louvre!–after getting engaged. The moment was perfect!

Neither of us were interested in a long, drawn-out engagement. We are more of the "take action now" type, so we decided to set our marriage date for April of the next year. This would give us about four months to put it all together.

On our path of dating and running a business together, we had our rough moments of disagreement and sometimes contention. We both wanted a wonderful, harmonious marriage, and knew it would be wise to seek outside counseling before we tied the knot. Both of our parents had divorced when we were younger, and we did not want to repeat that pattern. We found a Christian marriage counselor at the church we attended. He was just the right person to make us both feel comfortable.

It was at one of our counseling sessions that I felt it was time to let my dark secret out of the closet. Our pre-marriage counselor encouraged us to be open and share anything and everything we wanted the other one to know before we committed to each other "until death do us part, or forever hold our peace." He let us know that if we didn't, it would eat away at us in silence for the rest of our marriage. Jessica said she didn't have anything that she had not told me already, but obviously that was not the case for me. Our counselor did a good job of creating a safe environment where we could be totally honest, and I knew I had to confess that I had cheated on her in the very beginning of our relationship. With trepidation, I came clean and told her what I had done.

Jessica was beyond crushed. I could tell it hurt her so deeply that I thought it was over between us, with no chance of recovery. My pattern of self-sabotaging anything good in my life continued to haunt me. I slept on our couch for weeks. I reflected repeatedly how one stupid decision can instantly destroy all of the trust and good that had been built up over almost a year. I painfully remembered an analogy I had read in one of my self-development books.

It likened building trust to constructing a large dam that takes years of high-level engineering and masterful construction in order to separate massive bodies of water. One little crack or break in the dam can cause that entire body of water to explode through its borders in just a few hours. Ultimately, years of work can all be destroyed within a day due to one little break in the dam.

I apologized profusely every day, begging for Jessica to forgive me. I bought her flowers every week as a constant reminder of my unwavering commitment to our relationship. This went on for what seemed like an eternity. Over the next several weeks, she graciously forgave me, and agreed to still be married in April. While I am certainly not proud of the terribly poor decision I made, I can definitely say we are stronger because of it. My commitment to Jessica is even more rock solid. The whole event shook me up so much that I believe it cast out a weak part of who I was in my destructive past that obviously needed to be removed. Ironically, I am grateful for it, and have somehow found the good in it—although I would not recommend such selfish and careless behavior to anyone.

Amidst everything Jessica and I were experiencing together outside of our business, our marketing and sales company continued to thrive. We consistently closed a large number of deals every month, and our manager did an amazing job of running the operation without our constant supervision.

Before we knew it, April was upon us, and our wedding turned out to be a glorious event. We rented a luxurious yacht on Newport Bay, and we had a wonderful ceremony while floating on the water with our close family and friends. We were grateful that Joe and the entire family made it a priority to be there with us on this momentous occasion. It was easily one of the happiest days of my life, and a start to something incredible.

A Shift in the Business

Over time, the loan modification business began to plateau. There wasn't a lot of growth each month. We were losing passion for the industry, and it felt like the opportunity was shifting. We were still closing new deals, but not like previous months. A pivotal event caused us to rethink the whole business.

When we started hiring new sales reps in the beginning, I figured I would keep the company structure as simple as I could. I hired each new person as a 1099 subcontractor instead of as a W-2 employee. This proved to be detrimental in the end. After we let go of one of our sales reps, he applied for unemployment benefits with the state. This caused our corporation to be investigated and audited by the Employment Development Department of California. They found our company structure was not in accordance with California employment laws. We were fined a six-figure sum for back workers compensation fees, some penalties, and were mandated to reorganize the company.

I felt that destructive, negative force take a stab at my open wound once again, saying, "Are you ever going to learn how to not self-sabotage everything you build?"

We were at a crossroads with the whole situation, so we reached out to The CEO to seek further advice. Jessica and I sat in my office with Joe on speaker phone.

"Wow, sorry that happened *for* you all," Joe empathized.

Jessica turned to me and mouthed silently, "Did he just say happened *for* us?"

I nodded and referred her back to our *Lessons Learned* notebook, sitting on my desk. (See Chapter 4.)

"Skylar, did you know that structuring the company improperly was going to come back and bite you?" Joe asked pointedly.

I took a deep breath and felt like I was taking the witness stand in a courtroom. "I thought it would be okay just to do the 1099 thing—but it did cross my mind on several occasions. Now I realize I was playing too much in the gray area and should have gotten more clear on the proper set up," I admitted.

Joe seemed satisfied with my answer and continued, "Skylar, remember this. You've got to weigh the risk versus reward, or inevitably there will be penalties that can take you completely out of business."

Joe let that sink in for a moment and then said, "So, what's the plan now?"

"Umm, that's why we're calling you Joe. What would you do in this situation?" I responded.

"Well, first I would ask how the business is going and if you see a future in it. If the future looks bright and optimal, consider making the necessary structure change and continue on," Joe suggested.

"What if we don't see a future in it?" Jessica piped in.

"Then have the courage to move on. It's important to recognize the trends in temporary business opportunities so when the ship is sinking, you can get out. Likewise, it's wise to identify sustainable businesses that will be around no matter what the economy is doing. This loan modification game is slowing down and will likely end in the foreseeable future. You've taken advantage of the peak of it, and now it is heading towards the valley. I would negotiate the amount you owe the EDD and pay it, then consider selling the business," Joe concluded.

By the end of our call with Joe, Jessica had already noted down a lesson learned in our notebook.

LESSON #15: RISK VERSUS REWARD

You must always weigh the risk vs. reward, or inevitably there will be penalties that can take you completely out of business.

Jessica and I agreed with Joe's advice and decided to move on from Lewis Marketing. I negotiated a reduced fine with the EDD and sold the business to our manager, who wanted to continue with it.

We wanted a fresh start and some distance from the business we had run for 18 months, so we packed up our lives and moved back to Temecula, California. If you asked me if I thought our first million-dollar business was successful, I would have to tell you "yes and no." We learned a lot about how to simplify to scale, and literally created a million-dollar business from scratch. We broke through our own doubts and fears and figured out some secrets to marketing and scaling.

On the flip side, not playing by the rules took everything we had built and jeopardized it almost overnight. This crucial lesson has served me well ever since.

REVIEW AND EVALUATIONS OF LESSONS LEARNED

LESSON #15:

You must always weigh the risk versus reward of not playing by the rules.

Evaluate your current level of
"playing by the rules" in your business.
Circle your current, honest answer. 1 = Not at All and 5 = Absolutely

I know and play by the rules when it comes to my taxes.

1	2	3	4	5

I know and play by the rules when it comes to my company's legal structure.

1	2	3	4	5

My company knows and plays by the rules when it comes to employment law.

1	2	3	4	5

If your answers are less than a 5, what specific actions will you take to increase them to a level 5?

_____

_____

_____

_____

CHAPTER 9

THE LAUNCH OF A BRAND

Our minds were already thinking about what business we could start as we settled in our new place. We wanted to go with the more sustainable route this time—a business that was going to be around regardless of major shifts in the economy. While consulting with Joe about our new venture, he suggested we find something that had already been tried and tested and had a process we could just copy.

As we brainstormed, I thought of my dad's carpet-cleaning business that he had been operating in another city. Jessica and I discussed if this were something we could see ourselves doing. I knew it would be a physical-labor-intensive business unlike anything we were used to. However, I could leverage my marketing skills to surpass the competition in the outdated carpet-cleaning industry. She agreed to pursue it with me as long as she did not have to do the labor long-term.

I asked my dad if he would show us the ropes, and if he wouldn't mind if we started our own cleaning company in a different location. He agreed and was very gracious in demonstrating how all of the equipment worked and how to manage the day-to-day operation.

We recognized our initial investment in the carpet cleaning business was going to be much larger than $1000, but we had long since learned the formula of having to invest in order to get a return. Unlike the loan modification company, where all we needed was a cell phone, a computer, and a signed application, with carpet cleaning we had to purchase all the necessary equipment up front before we could start. We acquired a van and all the equipment needed. We also added window and house cleaning to our line of services as an additional way to maximize our value to the customer.

Jessica and I diving into our new carpet-cleaning business.

Within a few weeks, everything was primed and ready. Needless to say, we set up our company structure in order to "play by the rules." When it came to our business name, we wanted something that would emphasize a standard of excellence, so Superior Cleaning was the winner. Now all we needed were the customers.

Our budget was maxed out with the purchase of all the equipment, and we had very little to put towards our marketing efforts. We wanted to focus locally, and we needed customers as soon as possible. Jessica suggested we call Joe to see what his thoughts were on the matter.

Joe began, "I remember being in this very same situation when I started one of my companies. I knew eventually I would have a significant budget for marketing, but in the beginning, I took action on what I could do. I went out with just flyers and my business cards, and knocked on people's doors to acquire customers. Until the people came to me, I was willing to go out and bring in the customers."

"Joe, are you suggesting we literally go knock on doors to get business?" I asked, hoping he'd have another idea.

"That is correct, Skylar. Most small-to-medium-sized business owners fail in their next venture because they are not willing to do what it takes all over *again* to make the business work. You must be willing to do whatever it takes every time. Are you both willing to do that in the beginning to make it happen?" Joe asked.

I looked at Jessica, who firmly nodded her head, so we both answered, "Yes, of course!"

"Eventually you'll have a marketing budget again and be able to get your advertising machine working, although it will need to be a little different than your last business. You must see yourself as a marketer. This is one of the main hats you'll wear, and you've got to be willing to invest a significant amount of time and money into it. You could have the cure to cancer, but if no one knows about it, nobody gets the cure! I know you already know this based on your last business, but this is crucial," The CEO explained.

Jessica pushed the mute button on our phone and said to me, "Ask him what else he would do if he were in our shoes."

Feeling in a bit of a playful mood, I unmuted the phone and said, "Joe, Jessica has a question she wants to ask you."

She shook her head and backhanded me in the chest, but nonetheless proceeded with grace. "Hi, Joe, thank you so much for all of your help—it truly has been so amazing. You have been so giving of your time and knowledge to us. We hope to compensate you somehow for all of it."

"Of course, my pleasure, Jessica. You two are worth the effort! For now, my compensation is seeing you both succeed," Joe said.

"Well, we recognize your valuable mentorship, and we are sincerely grateful. Skylar and I were wondering how you would go about starting a new company you weren't super familiar with."

I was so grateful Jessica thought to ask that and was once again impressed with her people skills. She taught me a lesson on the importance of making others feel valued and special. As long as I have known her, she has freely expressed her gratitude to people and about things. It is truly a gift, and I could see her sharing that gift with the world on a grander scale somehow in the future.

As usual, Joe came through for us. "Just like you both did in the beginning of your marketing and sales company, I strongly suggest you perform the major roles in your new company so you understand firsthand what it takes to uphold a standard of excellence. Then when you hire someone to fill the role, it will come from a real place of intelligence. It shouldn't be forever—just for a short period until you feel it's time to replace yourself in each role. Many business owners get stuck here, feeling that they need to be the ones to do all or most of the work. They think they're saving money by not hiring a team, but this small-minded thinking often leads to unfulfillment, and certainly doesn't allow a life of liberty," Joe wisely taught us.

LESSON #16: DO WHATEVER IT TAKES

Most small to medium size business owners fail in their next business because they are not willing to do all that it takes all over again to make the business work. So they fail. You must be willing to do whatever takes every time.

LESSON #17: INVEST IN MARKETING

You must see yourself as a marketer as one of the main hats you wear, and be willing to invest a significant amount of time and money into it. Many businesses fail by not spending enough time or money on advertising and marketing. You could have the cure to cancer, but if no one knows about it, nobody gets the cure!

We made up some attractive flyers and set out to knock on doors to bring in some initial business. Jessica and I made it fun and enjoyed getting to talk with the people in our area. While it was not the marketing strategy of choice, we were determined to follow Joe's counsel and do whatever it took to create another successful company.

After a couple weeks of knocking on doors, the pump had been primed and the faucet was flowing. We were busy doing everything ourselves for the first three months, learning and performing each role. My dad proved helpful on many occasions when we had specific questions pertaining to the carpet-cleaning business.

We labored together intensively. I would mainly clean the carpets, and Jessica would clean the windows and other parts of the house. It was exhausting work, but we had a bigger vision to achieve. The next step in our plan came rather abruptly one day.

As we were cleaning a customer's house, Jessica emerged from the bathroom with her long rubber gloves and bucket of cleaning supplies. I thought she looked cute in all her work getup, but her face indicated she was not happy. "Skylar, I am never cleaning someone else's toilet again as long as I live! It's time for us to hire other people to do this."

I quickly got the point. We hired two technicians and purchased another van. We moved Jessica to the office to handle all the accounting and administration work. True to her word, she has never cleaned someone else's toilet again.

With our two technicians fully capable of doing the cleaning, I focused my efforts on sales, marketing, and the management of the business. I found a niche in internet marketing and built our website. I started working on ranking for organic Google traffic and arranged for pay-per-click advertising. It was a hefty investment, but I knew it would separate us from the competition. As Joe said, many others are not willing to put a significant amount of money and time into marketing. After a few months, the increase in leads and business allowed us to hire two more technicians and purchase two more operating vans. We doubled down on our internet marketing.

There was something else growing in our lives that caused us to find someone to replace Jessica in the office: we found out we were expecting our first child! We were so excited to be parents and start creating the family we both wanted. Yet there was so much Jessica did to make the business run smoothly, we wondered how we would find the right person.

I went to work searching on Craigslist for potential office manager candidates, and finally came across one named Holly who I felt could handle the job. Holly was sharp and savvy with her organization skills, and always seemed on top of taking calls and writing the invoices. We delegated everything we thought she could handle so Jessica could be home more preparing for our son.

Everything was humming along, and we were catching a glimpse of what life might look like with the right people running our business. We eventually hired a salesperson to do the estimates, two more technicians, and additional office staff. We now had 10 team members at Superior Cleaning. However, there was some reason for concern.

Despite all of our consistent cleaning jobs, our final profits didn't seem very strong. Looking back, I should have paid more attention to this in the moment to figure out why, but I figured it would eventually correct itself with more business coming in. So, we just kept plunging forward. Besides, there were other things now consuming my time.

Our first son, Brenden, was born during our Superior Cleaning journey, and I wanted to be at home as much as possible. Jessica was a wonderful wife, and now she glowed as a mother. I did not know you could love someone so much so instantly as when I first held our boy in my arms. We had started a couple of businesses together, but nothing compared to this human life we created. Brenden's birth instilled in us a new purpose and commitment to rise up to a higher level as parents. Nonetheless, I felt the constant pull towards running our business, which often limited my time at home.

My solution to this was, *If I bring in more business, it will solve all my problems.* It would allow us to be profitable, and the security of more money in our bank accounts would help me feel like I could spend ample time at home with my family. I felt like I was doing everything I could in marketing and sales, but I found myself working longer and longer hours to try to make up the difference. This put added stress on my relationship with Jessica. Instead of pleasant conversations late after work, we found ourselves arguing over the littlest things, and we were both exhausted in our respective roles as a business owner and a mother. Something had to change. I didn't have the solution, so I finally calmed my ego and called Joe for advice.

We started out our conversation about my concerns in my business, and Joe agreed that it sounded like I was doing everything right to make a profit in the carpet cleaning business, but then he broadened my perspective on some additional opportunities. We had become one of the premier carpet cleaning companies in our area and started collaborating with water and fire restoration companies as a subcontractor. Joe, who was in that very industry, suggested we do the whole restoration job when it presented itself—essentially, dry out a house when there was water damage. He alluded to the fact that I was just leaving money on the table. Then Joe intuitively asked how Jessica and I were doing with our new baby and with me working so many hours.

"Honestly, Joe, I feel like Jessica and I are growing further apart when all I want is to feel how it used to feel when we were dating and first married," I confessed.

"When was the last time you took Jessica on a date?" Joe asked with some force.

"It's been way too long. I can't even remember," I admitted.

"Skylar, of all the things worthy of your investment in both time and resources, your relationship with your spouse comes first. None of the business accolades you may achieve will compensate for failure in the home. Even though you have a child, you *must* continue to date your wife every single week. Give her something to count on and to look forward to—some time you both can focus on just each other and set aside everything else. Otherwise, you wake up one day as strangers living under the same roof. Karen and I schedule date nights every single week, and nothing takes priority over that. I want her to know she is my number one priority. Make sense?" Joe asked.

Joe's advice proved very beneficial, both on the business side and more importantly, on my relationship with Jessica. By taking on a few complete restoration jobs, I saw the vast increase we could make on a single opportunity. We had worked this business diligently for nearly

18 months, and I felt like Jessica and I were due for a little extended vacation. Perhaps I could make up for the lack of one-on-one time over the past several months.

Brenden was now a year old, and we felt comfortable leaving him with family for a few days, so we decided to go on a cruise to get away from it all and reconnect. We were able to step away from the business and let it run without us. This is what I had always wanted, but I can honestly say I was not fully relaxed. As we sat by the window in our tiny cruise ship room, I felt uneasy.

"Jessica, do you trust Holly 100%?" I asked.

"No, not 100%," she replied.

"There is something I just can't put my finger on. Babe, we can't have someone that we don't totally trust working for us. That doesn't sit right with me. It's going to be hard, but I think we need to let her go," I said determinedly.

Jessica begrudgingly agreed but felt the weight of having to train someone new to handle everything Holly was doing.

"Whatever it takes, right?" I reminded her as a life of liberty seemed to grow further away.

When we got back, we let Holly go. We also decided to shut down the cleaning company due to the small profits and shift our focus just on damage restoration jobs. We promoted our office assistant, Melissa, to office manager in place of Holly. A couple of weeks into her new role, she came into my office. I could tell she was stressed.

"I think Holly was embezzling from you," Melissa said.

I felt the blood leave my face. "How do you know?"

"I've been calling our customers to get payments, and they said they already paid us," she reluctantly responded.

As we dug deeper, we realized Holly had been stealing from us from the very beginning. She had created a PayPal account called Superior Cleaning and had asked customers to make final payments through PayPal. She would then revise the invoices to show a lower total amount. This was the reason we were not profitable! Too late now: we had already closed the cleaning company. How could I have let this happen?

"This isn't right," I told Jessica as we pulled up to the police station.

The heat from the southern California sun beat down on us as we walked up to the double glass doors. I opened the door and asked for the detective who had been assigned to our case. As we waited in the lobby, I still couldn't believe what had happened. Our world had been shaken to the core.

Detective Jones of the Lake Elsinore Police Department greeted us and walked us down the hallway to his office. We sat down, and the questioning began. "How long did you know Holly?"

"One year. We met her through posting a job on Craigslist," I answered.

"Did you ever suspect this was happening based on her behavior?" The detective continued.

"No. We were so comfortable with her that we even sometimes let her watch our one-year-old son," I admitted.

"Do you want to press charges?" he asked.

"Yes, we do!" Jessica quickly responded.

We sat there for a minute while he got the paperwork. Jessica's eyes started to tear up. I pulled her to my chest for a minute and softly said, "I am sorry about all of this."

We left the detective's office feeling a little better, hoping justice would be served. Little did we know about the lack of punishment when it comes to financial crimes.

I got a call from Mr. Jones shortly thereafter. "We found Holly and she is now in jail, but unfortunately she will only be there for one day."

"What? Why is that?" I asked, perplexed.

"People convicted of financial crimes don't do much time. She will have this on her record for the rest of her life, though. Unfortunately, that's just the way the system works," he explained.

Justice was never really served, but I was served in another way. I was distraught about the whole injustice factor, and I felt myself getting more and more fired up with anger and destructive thoughts. I needed to talk it out with someone, so I called Joe.

"Hey, Joe, sorry about the short notice on this, but can I meet you somewhere? Are you in town?" I asked hopefully.

"Sure, Skylar, are you doing okay, what's going on?" Joe asked with a concerned voice.

"I would rather just talk to you in person about it, if that's okay? I am happy to drive to wherever you are right now," I said willingly.

We agreed to meet at a coffee shop close to where Joe was. It was about an hour's drive, and my thoughts were raging inside. I was full of feelings of being taken advantage of and of being the victims of such an awful crime. Jessica and I felt violated. Tens of thousands of dollars of rightfully earned money were just flat out gone! On top of that, we shut down the entire cleaning company based on the low profits. As I pulled up to the coffee shop, all my focus was on blaming Holly.

After exchanging pleasantries with Joe, I got right to the point. "Our previous office manager embezzled a ton of money from us right under our noses. She oversaw all of our accounts payable and receivable, and she had our customers pay to an account she had set up on the side instead of to our company account. This is why our carpet cleaning business failed. We were taken advantage of Joe!"

I was breathing heavily and practically yelling the details to Joe, who was only a few feet in front of me at our little cafe table. The CEO leaned back in his chair with his arms folded, probably to guard himself from my fiery remarks and lit-up temper.

I softened my tone a little but continued to vent. "We finally felt like we got something really good going, but this girl took it from us. It's not our fault profits were so low—she was stealing them."

My mentor sat patient and silent, waiting for me to simmer down. His lips were tightly pressed and he was slowly nodding his head, taking in all of the details. For once, I thought it was not me who self-sabotaged this whole mess—it was Holly.

"Skylar, my friend, I can appreciate your anger and ill feelings towards Holly. Truly. However, I am also grateful this happened *for* you," Joe said, attempting to console me.

I felt a valuable lesson coming on, but my pride and ego were all-consuming and put up a blockade. For once, I did not feel like I wanted to hear it. Joe noticed me rolling my eyes and my body language rejecting whatever his advice was about to be. I put my elbows on the little table and buried my face in my hands to avoid eye contact.

"I can see you are too distraught and not ready to hear what I am about to tell you, Skylar, so why don't you call me when you've settled down a bit."

This is not what I wanted. I actually *did* want to hear what Joe had to say about the whole matter, but that negative force that had plagued me so many times throughout my life had a different type of grip on me this time. I even brought along my *Lessons Learned* notebook with the intention to take in his advice. Regardless, Joe stood up from his chair and started to leave.

"No, please don't leave! I apologize for not being willing to listen. I drove all of this way so I could hear what you have to say. Please stay. I am ready to receive it now," I pleaded humbly.

Joe took a deep breath and stared at me sitting hopelessly in my chair. My mind flashed back to our very first encounter: me standing in front of him with my hands cuffed behind my back in his restaurant parking lot, and him having mercy on me. Maybe he thought of the same memory, because he slowly returned to his seat and decided to stay. I immediately surrendered any prideful or egotistic thoughts and sat patiently waiting for his advice.

"Tell me, who hired Holly in the first place?" Joe questioned with a tone that was gentle yet pointed.

I gulped and said, "I did."

"Did you do a background check on her?"

"No."

"Did you have checks and balances in place to protect you from embezzlement?"

"No."

"Were you regularly reviewing the accounts receivables and comparing collections to the bank accounts?"

"No."

"Did you keep her on board for an extended time even though you didn't fully trust her?"

"Yes."

"Then take responsibility for your actions. You brought her on board, and you kept her on even though neither you nor Jessica fully trusted her. You are cursing and blaming her for your losses, and as a result you have taken the victim mentality. There is no progression in this path, Skylar, none! When you decide to lose your hate and your blame, you will find your peace. However, you cannot have both at the same time, because they do not live in the same space," Joe counseled. This was a huge idea and difficult for me to take in all at once.

He continued, "Skylar, with most of the circumstances in my life that cause me pain or frustration, I find a way to come from a place of responsibility instead of victimhood. I get to make that choice. Now you get to make that choice, and you will feel the emotions that come with that choice. *I can almost always find some way that I had some level of responsibility in any situation or circumstance.* It doesn't mean it's always my fault, but it does mean that I have some responsibility in the outcome. This has allowed me to live in peace most of my life while others stay frustrated and resentful—sometimes until the day they die."

LESSON #18: TAKE RESPONSIBILITY

When you decide to lose your hate and your blame, you will find your peace. The faster you take responsibility for *everything* in your life, the faster you will have total control of your life.

REVIEW AND EVALUATIONS OF LESSONS LEARNED

LESSON #16:

Most small to medium size business owners fail in their next business because they are not willing to do all that it takes all over again to make the business work. So they fail. You must be willing to do whatever takes every time.

What are the things in your business you know you should be doing, but aren't?

_____

_____

_____

_____

LESSON #17:

You must see yourself as a marketer. Many businesses fail by not spending enough time or money on advertising and marketing. You could have the cure to cancer, but if no one knows about it, nobody gets the cure!

We have all the leads and new business we can handle.

1	2	3	4	5

We have a significant budget for marketing and advertising.

1	2	3	4	5

Our marketing strategy is effective and
bringing in all the business we can handle.

1	2	3	4	5

If your answers are less than a 5,
what specific actions can you take to increase them to a level 5?

_____

_____

_____

_____

LESSON #18:

When you decide to lose your hate and your blame, you will find your peace. The faster you take responsibility for *everything* in your life, the faster you will have total control of your life.

Circle your current, honest answer. 1 = Not at All and 5 = Always

I take personal responsibility for *all* issues within my business.

1	2	3	4	5

I take personal responsibility for the results (or lack of results) in my life by not blaming others.

1   2   3   4   5

I do not blame anyone for anything that is not how I want it in my life.

1   2   3   4   5

If your answers are less than a 5,
what specific actions can you take to increase them to a level 5?

_____

_____

_____

_____

CHAPTER 10

IT ALL STARTS WITH YOU

Our new company, Superior Restoration, was officially born in 2012 as we shifted all our focus to water and fire damage restoration. We were able to keep most of our existing team and move forward. We did our best to apply the lessons learned along the way, and we became fairly successful.

Within a two-year period, we went from four trucks to ten. We grew to a team of twenty-two, and profits were good. We bought a beautiful house on five acres with a pool —but we were so busy we couldn't fully enjoy it. We were scaling quickly, but I did not have all the tools necessary to keep the wheels on, and things were getting wobbly. Nonetheless, I felt like I knew what I was doing, so I just kept plunging forward, hoping someday I would create the same life Joe had.

The business was now at $3,000,000 in revenue, and I was feeling confident in my abilities. But somehow, I let pride and egotism enter my life again, and instead of seeking out The CEO's advice, I wanted to show him that Jessica and I could run our business just as well, if not better, than him. Maybe it was because I wanted her to see me as the hero, or maybe I was trying to still rebuild and prove to her that I was worthy of her trust.

Superior Restoration team in 2014.

Time passed, and I felt ashamed and embarrassed to reach out to my longtime mentor. We would occasionally check in with a cordial greeting, but regretfully, nothing more than that.

One day, I realized I was creating a business and life that was the opposite of what Jessica and I wanted. I was still working long hours and spending less time at home with our family. Our second precious son, Jeremiah, was born after two years of running Superior Restoration, and I felt like I was getting further and further away from being an incredible father and amazing husband. I still found a way to squeeze in a date with Jessica once a week, but we could both feel it was just transactional. My natural inclination and historic pattern was to run away from it all—or sell the company and move on to something else easier, perhaps.

We constantly had challenges with our business and team members. There was so much conflict amongst our team—and myself, for that matter. My heart was not in it anymore, and almost daily I was looking for a way to get out. One day, that all shifted abruptly with a literal smack in the face.

"What happened to your face?" asked Mike one Monday morning at the office.

"What do you mean?" I replied.

"The whole left side of your face is scraped," he observed.

I stood there with an embarrassed look on my face. "You don't want to know," I replied.

That weekend, we had our year-end holiday party, and Mike had not been able to attend. I had it at our newly purchased 5,500-square-foot house, and I wanted to show all of our team members and their spouses a good time in an attempt to somehow make things better. I loaded the tables with enough alcohol for a college frat party. As the night went on, the bottles started emptying. One of our team members had a funny laugh, and I loved hearing it. So, wise CEO I was, I thought it would be funny to start chasing him around the house while tickling him. As I ran full speed through our double doors to our outside patio, my foot snagged on the bean bag toss game, and I slid face-first onto the concrete. As I got to my feet, Jessica glared at me with disappointment and concern as blood dripped down the side of my face.

The first quarter of the next year, our top-producing team member and manager, who was responsible for the most revenue in the company, locked in a very large hospital remediation job. He and his team worked all day on it and were making major progress. That next morning, I received a troubling call from him. "Last night, I took the guys out to a bar and Chris got pretty hammered. He ended up going back to the hotel and fell asleep in the bathtub. He left the water running and it flooded the hotel. He is okay, though..."

I was horrified by the news, and it was the final tipping point. Our team was dysfunctional, and many times impossible to deal with. I was done! I got in my car and drove home to tell Jessica I was going to sell the company and we were moving on to something else. To validate my decision, I explained to her what had happened with Chris getting drunk. Her answer was not what I expected.

"It looks like your people are following in your footsteps," Jessica pointed out.

"What is that supposed to mean?" I asked defensively.

"I mean just a couple months ago, you taught everyone that it was okay to get drunk and act like lunatics right here in our house. It sounds like they are just doing what you authorized them to do!" she fired back.

Her accusation stopped me in my tracks and silenced me. There was nowhere I could go with it. As hard as it was to swallow, she was right. Seeing a little humility on my face, Jessica continued.

"Skylar, I know things have been tough and you want to sell the business. I am on your team and I will support you, but can I ask that you do one thing before you make that decision?"

I wasn't sure where she was going, but I nodded my head.

Seeing she had a green light, Jessica continued in a calmer yet assertive voice, "Please call Joe and ask for his advice. I know you have been doing your best on your own for the last few years, but we are obviously not where we want to be, and especially have not achieved anywhere near what he has. Let go of your pride, babe, and just reach out to him first before you sell the company."

She handed me our *Lessons Learned* notebook to help me remember what it was we were going for. The ball was in my court.

I obviously knew what the right thing to do was, and I agreed to speak with Joe before I made any drastic decisions. I reflected on my communication, or the lack thereof, with The CEO over the past year or so. It was sparse, and I noticed on our text threads that it was mostly Joe who initiated our conversations and check-ins. After a while it just fizzled, and why wouldn't it? I was no longer actively seeking his advice when I probably really needed it. I, too, would stop putting energy towards someone that showed less and less appreciation for my time.

Not wanting to overthink myself out of making the phone call to Joe, I took immediate action. With every passing ring, I conjured up in my mind what I would say. Finally, on what seemed like the last ring before it went to voicemail, Joe answered.

"Well look who it is, my long-lost friend Skylar Lewis!" Joe started in with some obviously pointed energy on the fact that I had not been consistent in reaching out to him.

In a repentant tone, I started in. "Hey Joe, thank you for picking up. I know I have not been good about connecting with you for a while, and I sincerely apologize for that."

Joe was silent for a long moment while I endured waiting for his response. "It's all right, Skylar. I am sure there is a reason, but I am not interested in hearing that reason because it will probably just be an excuse. Over time I've developed an immunization to this excuse disease. I don't validate them for people anymore. So what's going on in your world?"

"My business has been going downhill for a while despite my efforts to improve. We hit three million in revenue this year, but my team members are not performing at a high level, and our company's morale is stifling. I purposely avoid coming into the office some days. I want to sell the business and get out, but I wanted to check in with you first to get your advice," I explained.

"Hmm, that's interesting. We are both in the same industry, and yet my company has consistently increased in profit every year for the last six years. Our company morale is very high, and our team members are performing at a very high level. What do you think the difference is, Skylar?" Joe asked.

I allowed his statement to add insult to my injury, but something happened inside of me that caused me to dig deeper. It was as if his aggravating my exposed wound increased my capacity to a new level. Like our muscles, they must be broken down first in order to be built up stronger. The fact is, I did not know what the difference was—why Joe's company was so successful and mine was not—but I was willing to do what it took to find out. A second wind of hope entered my being – maybe it was possible to course correct our sinking company ship.

"Joe, can I come visit you at your company headquarters to see how you do things?" I asked with sincere hope.

"I will agree to meet with you, but the terms are going to be different moving forward. The stakes just got higher. Meet me at my company office tomorrow morning at 8:00 a.m., and we'll discuss the details. I'll text you the address," Joe stated.

I agreed, not knowing Joe's office was a solid two hours away from me. Nonetheless, I was willing to go the distance to fix the problems, while still considering selling my company.

The next morning, I was greeted at the front desk by a sharp, kind receptionist. As I sat in the lobby, I noticed friendly faces going in and out with upbeat conversations. Everyone that walked by asked if I had been helped. The receptionist led me to a seat in the conference room and said that Joe would be there shortly. I immediately noticed how I felt at his operation. Team members seemed happy and driven with purpose. My mind reflected back to my association with his team members over

10 years ago at his restaurant. I had somehow forgotten how everyone was on point and performed with a standard of excellence.

Joe entered the room, and I instinctively rose to my feet and gave him a hug. It had been a couple of years since our last meeting, but once we were together, it seemed like it was just yesterday. We sat down, and after exchanging some pleasantries and Joe asking about my growing family, he got right to the point.

"Skylar, up to this point I have mentored you along your path. I have helped you through some tough times and taught you some basic yet essential things on how to run a successful business. From this point forward we will always remain dear friends. However, if you want me to coach you, it's going to require some skin in the game. How much money have you invested in yourself by going to business seminars, paying for coaches, or investing in self-development?" Joe asked.

"I haven't really done any of that. I've been too busy running my company," I responded, hoping it was a valid reason.

"This is exactly why you are in the position you are in, my friend. You must always be sharpening the saw, Skylar, or it will quickly go dull. Abraham Lincoln brilliantly stated it this way: "*Give me six hours to chop down a tree, and I will spend the first four sharpening the saw.*"

Joe continued, "How do you think I got to where I am so fast?"

The question was rhetorical. Obviously, Joe had invested a significant amount into himself to cut the learning curve and stay sharp in business and in life. Then he decided to put me to the test.

"Skylar, now you must be willing to invest in yourself. For me to agree to coach you through this, it will cost $25,000. While I don't need the money, if I am going to pour my time and energy into you and hold you accountable at a high level, it will only be in your best interest to make an investment. Frankly, I know the value is ten times that investment.

Many people go through life magically expecting a return when no investment has been made. So, are you ready to rise up, Skylar, and make this happen?" Joe asked.

Joe's proposal stretched my thinking. It was another moment to evaluate if the desired goal and reward was larger than the fear of what was potentially holding me back. I knew we had the money, and I knew we desperately needed help. I sat up straight and determined to somehow shake off the weak man inside of me that had self-sabotaged so much of my life up to that point.

"I'm all in, Joe," I declared.

"No more playing small and staying comfortable?" Joe tested me.

"No more playing small and staying comfortable!" I stated with conviction.

"And Skylar, when I say staying comfortable, I am referring to all the major areas of your life. No more playing small in your faith, family, fitness or finances. You must learn to create results simultaneously in each of those four foundational pillars. I will not work with you if you only want to create success in business. It will never be worth it to sacrifice the relationship with your wife and kids for business success. Candidly, at the end of the day, life is not about business success; it's about the impact you have made on the people around you. I can honestly and undeniably attribute the achievements in my life to the simple fact that I have been intentional about investing in each of those four pillars on a daily basis. You must commit to rising up in all of them if you want to work with me."

Joe was silent after presenting me with his ultimatum. I knew he was right, and he obviously recognized I was majorly out of balance in those four foundational pillars in my life. I felt a new measure of courage bubble up inside of me, so I looked Joe in the eyes with determination and confidently said, "I agree, and I am committed to invest and significantly improve all four pillars in my life."

"I was hoping you would, Skylar. Then I will agree to coach you." Joe extended his hand to solidify our agreement.

Joe wasted no time and started in with his coaching. "In my hand is a guidebook on how to become a 2-Day-CEO. It's the same book I've shared parts of with you and Jessica. It is derived from years of experience and proving systems and processes. It flat out works, but I cannot do the work for you. One man cannot do another man's push-ups for him. Do you understand?"

"Yes, Joe, I'm willing to do the work," I affirmed.

"Great! Then let's start with the reason why your business is not where you want it to be," Joe began.

With my *Lessons Learned* notebook open to a fresh page I was ready to write down whatever The CEO taught me. "Write this down word for word, Skylar. The reason my business is not where I want it to be is because of me."

I looked up with my eyebrows raised, questioning what Joe just told me.

"Go ahead, write it down. That's the fact of the matter," Joe directed.

Wanting to be obedient and coachable, I reluctantly wrote down that *I was the reason why my business was not where I wanted it to be*, then looked up for more instructions.

Noticing my submission and willingness, Joe said, "You will have a very difficult time getting the business to grow profitably and operate without you if you are not aware of your own weaknesses. You are the leader of the organization, and you set the pace for everyone until you find a replacement leader who will take over that task. Your weaknesses typically become your team member's weaknesses. If you miss meetings, they will miss meetings. If you're late, they will start to be late. If you have integrity issues, they will have integrity issues."

While it was certainly tough to swallow, what Joe just said made sense. Humble Pie had been served, and it was not a side dish, it was the main course.

Joe continued, "Your organization will model you. The core values of an organization always start from the top—you—and work their way down. What you value becomes what the organization values. If you value hard work, the organization will value hard work. If you value treating people fairly, so will your team members. I cannot understate how important it is that you become the best version of yourself for your company. The little things you do 'wrong' matter. Your team is watching your every move." I swallowed, thinking of what kind of a model I'd been to my business.

Joe kept up his indicting lecture. "I've seen firsthand that the chaos in an organization always stems from the leader. The leaders of these organizations have blind spots they cannot see. The blind spots lead to dysfunction within the team, which inevitably leads to a business filled with chaos, strife, and profits that are lower than expected."

Joe handed me a full copy of his guidebook and pointed out the page he wanted me to focus on. He advised me to use it not only as a guidebook, but as a workbook.

Here are some solutions to YOU being the problem:

1. Hire an executive coach to help point out your blind spots.
2. Read some books on self-awareness and attend personal development seminars.

3. Develop a culture where direct and honest feedback becomes a part of your team's DNA, especially when it comes to feedback for the CEO.

"You have already committed to the first solution and parts of the second, so focus on solution 3. Our arrangement going forward is we will set our next meeting time according to the time frame needed to implement the principles in the guidebook, and we will adjust that time frame as needed. To get moving quickly, let's meet next week at this same time. Get to work and focus on the solutions listed so we can move into the next steps.

"I'll leave you with one more task before you go. You must become aware of how you are showing up and how your team sees you. You can start this process by taking a personality assessment. There are many out there, but I use the DISC assessment. Take this assessment and then review the report to get an understanding of how others see you."

To learn more about personality assessments for you and your team, go to www.2dayceo.com/resources/disc

As I left his office, I sincerely thanked Joe for his willingness to be my coach. A surge of hope came over me that maybe it was possible to rescue my company from the downward spiral it was currently on and get it to a place worthy of selling.

Back at my office, I reviewed the solutions again and went to work. I had just taken action on the first solution by hiring Joe as my coach. For the second solution, I recognized I had let my reading habit slack for some time, so I committed to read a self-help book each month. I had not attended a business seminar for many years but thought maybe Joe's coaching would fill that purpose for now. With that in mind, I dove into solutions 3 and 4.

SOLUTION #3:
A CULTURE OF DIRECT AND HONEST FEEDBACK

One of the top reasons organizations struggle internally is due to the lack of direct and honest feedback. Whether it be positive recognition for an achievement or constructive criticism on something that can be improved, a strong practice of open and honest feedback significantly boosts any organization's overall culture of accountability and honesty. If you are not growing, you are stagnant, which leads to dying, and feedback serves as the fertilizer to nurture the company.

Your company is going to make mistakes—that's inevitable. The key is to have a system in place to collect feedback and correct the issues. A simple system to effectively obtain feedback from your organization is through a Working/Not Working item on most of your agendas.

We regularly ask our team what is working and what is not working in all areas of the business, including the people. When your team members feel they have a safe space to express themselves, they feel more valued, and inevitably increase their performance. Some of the best ideas will come from your own people; they just need a green light and a systematic platform to share it.

I also recommend doing a team member feedback survey once a quarter. You can have your team members fill it out anonymously if they so choose. This provides great feedback for the company and also shows the level of engagement from your team.

Obviously, you will not be able to change and adhere to every recommendation made. You and your executive team will have to evaluate each one and determine if it is in the team's and company's best interest. The consistent practice of letting the team members be heard breeds an empowering environment.

The CEO's advice caused me to do some serious self-reflection as a leader. I considered myself a "nice guy." I drove my team hard and could be demanding, but I definitely avoided conflict. This served me when it was just my friends and a small group of team members. As our company grew, it became increasingly more evident that we were "too nice" to each other. We did not want to ruffle each other's feathers—and now I see how our progress and growth was stunted.

I read Ray Dalio's book *Principles*. One of the things Ray talks about is being *radically truthful*. By avoiding conflict through not saying what needs to be said, one avoids resolving differences. We needed a major change in the way we perceived conflict so we could move through the differences we had as a team.

I wanted to get things moving quickly, so the next day I arranged an emergency meeting with our team and let them know it was time for us to address conflict head on. If they felt at odds about a decision made within our company, it was their responsibility to speak up. I also gave them permission to be more direct with each other, and especially me. I must admit I was a little naive to how this was going to shake out. My team members let it rip with no reservations and being criticized openly was extremely uncomfortable. It hurt. I chose to not let it make me angry, however, trusting Joe that tolerating the pain of it all would allow me to get to the next level in my leadership.

I wanted some specific feedback for me, so I sent out a team member survey asking how they would rate their CEO on the following:

1. Do I follow through with my commitments?

2. Do I operate in integrity?

3. Do I have a great attitude?

4. How well do I live and demonstrate our core values?

5. Where can I improve?

The result was like a swift kick in the groin. Some of my team thought I was out of integrity and I didn't follow through with my commitments. I was initially very angry, and wanted to show the team how bad a leader could really be. But once I got over myself, I realized that whether I felt I was out of integrity, some of my team saw me this way. Their perception of their leader was all that really mattered. I went to work and made a lifelong commitment to be open to feedback and to continually work on myself as a leader.

I thoroughly answered each question The CEO proposed, and it opened my understanding to the importance of these core traits of a successful leader. While completing the work in this section, I felt myself becoming more and more like the person I wanted my people to be, instead of expecting them to be someone more than I was willing to rise to myself. Once again, Joe was spot on: it all starts with *you* as the leader!

CHAPTER 11

MOVE OUT OF THE WAY— YOUR ROLE AS CEO

The next week came quickly, and before I knew it I was at Joe's office again ready to be coached. I could already feel a noticeable shift in my ability as a leader just by becoming aware and having the courage to give and receive direct and honest feedback with my team.

"Welcome back, Skylar. You seem more excited to be here this time," The CEO greeted me with a chuckle in his voice.

"Yes sir, I am ready and committed to do whatever it takes, and that last section you gave me has already had a huge impact!" I responded.

"Did you implement everything I outlined?" Joe inquired.

"I did, every part of it!"

Joe peered into my eyes in silence as if to test the integrity of my answer. "Good. Well done, Skylar. I ask because there is a common disease among business owners and leaders called FTI, and I wanted to make sure you didn't catch it."

"FTI? What's that?" I asked.

"Like I said, it's a disease that can be pretty devastating and crippling. It is no respecter of persons and will take down any business if you're not careful," Joe continued.

"With all due respect, Joe, I am still not sure what FTI stands for," I reminded him.

"It stands for *Failure to Implement*. A successful businessman, Howard Partridge, wrote a whole book on it. One can know everything they are supposed to do, but if they do not take action, nothing will happen. So, all of this will be for naught if you fail to implement. Understood?"

"Yes, understood. I see that the antidote or cure to FTI is immediate action," I affirmed.

"That's right. Now let's move on to the next section. Take out your guidebook and let's look at another key element to becoming a 2-Day-CEO," Joe said, instructing me to read aloud.

Move Out of the Way

You do not need to be involved in every decision at your company! The goal is that you are involved in very few decisions. You are slowing down your company if you need to be involved in many day-to-day decisions. It took me eight years to finally let go of ordering business cards. I always wanted to make sure the business cards were done right because of my expertise in marketing. However, that was a $20-an-hour job. The way I see it, you should not be doing anything that would take someone $50 or less to do. For medium-to-large companies, you shouldn't be doing anything under $250 to $500 an hour. Ask yourself the question, "Could someone else do this?" If so, give it to them or hire someone to do it. When you are involved in most of the decision making, it creates a bottleneck within your organization.

Your team eventually will feel like you do not trust them if you continue to give input and want to be involved in every decision. This hinders their growth as leaders and the growth of the business. Your team needs to make mistakes in order to rise to their next level. In order for your business to achieve the next level, it also needs leaders who can make decisions on their own.

A common tendency is for the leader to feel they have to express their expertise in certain circumstances. This can be a hindrance. To make this work, you must become the least valuable person in the company, rather than believing "I am the best at this and therefore I need to be involved in those decisions."

What decisions are you currently making that can be relinquished to your team?

_____

_____

_____

_____

_____

Joe allowed me some time to answer the question. This simple exercise immediately gave me a sense of relief and more brain space. I knew that once I empowered my managers and people to make more decisions without me, they would feel my level of trust in them increase. I had been holding on to far too many aspects of the business that could easily be done without me. His statement about me needing to be the least valuable person in the company was a definite mindset shift.

Joe found a page in the notebook and pointed at it. "Skylar, these are the roles of a CEO," Joe said.

CEO Roles

In the startup phase of any company you build, you will be handling almost everything. However, as your company progresses, you must start to pull yourself away from the routine tasks of the company. As you do this, it will free up time to focus on working on the business instead of *in* the business. You will eventually get to a point where you have people you trust running your company. When you get to that point, there are seven top things you need to manage/oversee as the CEO.

1. **Micromanage company culture.** You must be directly involved in creating the company culture and core values. Once they are developed, you must oversee the culture and micromanage it. Visit with your team members regularly, take them out to lunch, etc. Get a feel for where they are at mentally and emotionally. Run annual or semi-annual team member surveys with questions related to their engagement and how they feel about the company.

2. **Set the company's vision and top priorities.** You must be the one to set the company's direction and top priorities. The obvious priorities may be revenue and profitability. Other priorities may include community involvement, company-wide improvements in systems and processes, branding, etc.

3. **Own the key relationships.** In Mark Moses' book *Make Big Happen*, he describes the key relationships a CEO must own like this: "A key relationship is any relationship that would cause a great deal

of harm to your company if it went away, including key accounts, key customers, key vendors, and key banking relationships."

4. **Be involved in the hiring of key team members.** Always be involved in the hiring decision of any key team members. All team members are valuable, but some have more influence over your organization. For these, I recommend being involved in the interview process and really getting a feel for them. This also gives you time to build a relationship with them. If you are only working two days a week, making the final decision on key team members and having a relationship with them is critical.

5. **Review financial reports and key metrics.** As the CEO, you must know your numbers. You must fully understand them and know what drives them: key metrics. I recommend reviewing key metrics on a weekly basis and financial reports (P&L/Income statement, balance sheet, cash flow statement) on a monthly basis.

6. **Be involved in key company decisions**. These include anything that will dramatically change your company or put your company at risk. This may include changes to company policies, hiring practices, changes in key processes, changes in software, new key initiatives, etc.

7. **Oversee the system.** An important part of your job is making sure the system that runs your company is running efficiently. This includes all of your processes in each department. I recommend having some reports that show if any balls are being dropped or anything is missed, which will warn about any breakdown of your system. Once you identify this, immediately get with your operations team to remedy it. A stronger operations person/team usually leads to fewer breakdowns in the system.

As I reviewed the CEO Roles, a feeling of overwhelm came over me. "Joe, how am I going to wear all of these hats plus the other hats I am wearing? I am already too busy, and I don't want to take any other time away from Jessica and the kids," I said.

"Skylar, this is not a game of just adding more onto your plate. You must remove things from your plate by learning to delegate properly. This is a learned skill and an art that I will teach you," Joe said, as he directed me to read the next section in his guidebook.

How to Delegate so You, the CEO, Can Focus on the Most Important Tasks

Delegate: "To entrust a task or responsibility to another person." Sounds easy, right? Why do so many people struggle to implement this?

I say with confidence that one of the main reasons CEOs fail to get out of their business is they lack the skill set of delegation. Yes, delegation is a skill. To delegate properly, you must be:

- An exceptional communicator
- An exceptional trainer
- Exceptional at follow up

Your ability to delegate tasks to capable team members is in direct proportion to the amount of freedom you will have.

To be clear on what delegation is not: delegation is not handing a task off to someone else and hoping they will do it.

My working definition of delegation: "Clearly defining what needs to be done, properly training the person how to do it, and following up until you are confident they are doing it consistently and correctly."

Your primary goal as a CEO or leader of your company is to delegate as much as possible to give you room to focus on your roles as the CEO.

Here is a simple process of delegation.

Step #1: Write down everything you do.

Write down a list of everything you do at the company on a spreadsheet. *Everything*. Every little task. Examples: Answering the phone when a customer calls, handling customer complaints, ordering business cards, taking out the trash, talking with accounts, making sales calls, one-on-ones with team members, etc. There will usually be a list of 30 to 100+ things.

Step #2: Delegate your tasks.

It's time to delegate! To effectively do so, you must be very clear on what the person is going to be doing and how to do it. Many times, writing this out is the most effective way. Once you are clear on what the person is going to do, train them. Once you train them, you must follow up to verify the task is still being completed.

The Delegator's Mindset

Your role as the CEO/Leader is to delegate as much as you possibly can to the team members that are competent to handle the tasks. Consider everything that you do in the company as a temporary assignment. Learn that temporary assignment, master it, and then hand it off to a capable person. This is how you get out of the business. This one mindset shift can be a major game-changer for you.

Your job is not to be the expert. You want your *team* to be the experts. Give the praise to your team. Ask them how they would handle the specific challenge at hand. Step away from trying to solve everything (or even *anything*, if possible). Defer to your team whenever you can.

If there is a new task that needs to be done and no one else can do it, take it on with the intention of handing it back over to someone in the near future. Your eventual job description will be only the roles of the CEO described above. *You need to be focused more on strategy (working on the business) than being tactical (working in the business).*

To make this easy for you to implement, follow this structure:

Create three columns on a spreadsheet, and label the left column Task, the middle one Delegate, Keep, or Eliminate, and the right column Who.

As you identify your different Tasks in the first column, note in the center column if you are going to Delegate, Keep, or Eliminate the task by putting the letter D, K, or E.

Here is an example of how this looks:

A	B	C
Task	Delegate? D, K, E	Who?
Follow up on sales orders	D	John
Make welcome calls to customers	D	Jennifer
Review financials monthly	K	Me
Review weekly metrics	K	Me
Design business cards	E	Eliminate
Enter sales orders into system	D	Jennifer

D for Delegate. In the Who section, put the name of the person you are going to delegate this to. Tip: If there are a significant number of tasks you are delegating to one person, do it over time. Do not overwhelm them. When thinking about who to hand the task over to, understand that many times, they will not do it as well as you do. However, the only path to freedom is by delegating these tasks. *A good rule is if the team member can do the task 80% as well as you, that is sufficient.* This will not always work, but it will most of the time.

K for Keep. These are tasks that only you can do. No one else in the company is able to do these. These tasks are a high-level CEO function. Do not keep tasks just because you are good at them and think other people will not be able to do them. You might be surprised how other people can do your tasks just as well as you—and sometimes even better.

E for Eliminate. These are the tasks that don't really need to be done. They are time wasters.

Take a few minutes and start the process now.

Task	Delegate, Keep, or Eliminate?	Who

The instructions were straightforward, and Joe and I discussed how I was going to implement them in my company. He reached over to his multi-channeled conference speakerphone and asked one of his administrative staff to bring in an envelope laying on top of his desk. Once Joe had the envelope in his hand, he set it on the table and asked, "What are you doing next weekend?"

"I'm sure we don't have any specific plans, other than to be home with our boys," I answered, wondering why he would ask.

"Okay, can you get Jessica on speakerphone? I have a question I'd like to ask her," Joe asked assertively.

I did as I was instructed, and after the first ring, Jessica answered. "Hi babe, I'm here with Joe, and he wants to ask you a question."

"Hi Jessica, how are you and the boys doing?" Joe politely asked.

"We are doing great, thanks for asking, and thank you for whipping Skylar into shape," she said without a hint of irony.

"Believe me, it's my pleasure. I wanted to have Skylar call you because I wanted to see if you'd be ok if he accompanied me to a business seminar next weekend," Joe asked.

"Sure, Joe, where is it?" Jessica inquired.

"It's in Austin, Texas, with a pretty decent business guy named Keith Cunningham," Joe said

"That sounds amazing. Yes, I am totally good with that, and thanks for asking," Jessica concluded.

I sat in my chair around Joe's executive table with my eyes wide. Joe explained that I would have to buy my $5k ticket if I really wanted to go. The money seemed like a null point compared to what the opportunity afforded. I was curious why Joe would want to go to another seminar, though.

"Joe, you've been to so many seminars and events over the years. Why do you need to go to another one? Is there a point when you're ever done?" I inquired.

Joe got serious, looked me in the eyes, and said, "Skylar, you are never done investing in yourself, ever! As long as you and I are breathing, we'll be finding ways to get better. That's what the best leaders do. Understood?"

"Yes sir, I understand, but of all the seminars we could go to, why this one? This guy is not in our industry. How is this going to help our businesses?" I naively asked.

"That is a fair question, Skylar. You are right that he does not work in the same industry. However, he is a master at building machines that function with little effort once in place. He has figured out how to build brilliant systems, and that is a key element for you to learn and for me to continue to improve upon," The CEO explained.

REVIEW AND EVALUATIONS OF LESSONS LEARNED

To effectively lead as the CEO, you must master delegation.
Circle your current, honest answer. 1 = Not at All and 5 = Always

I operate with a delegator's mindset.

1	2	3	4	5

I regularly delegate tasks that are not "CEO" tasks.

1	2	3	4	5

I spend time thinking strategically about my business.

1	2	3	4	5

For any answer that is not a 5,
what specific actions can you take to improve? ?

_____

_____

_____

_____

PART TWO

THE FOUR PILLAR FRAMEWORK

Over the course of the next week and a half, I noted all my tasks and identified which ones I was going to keep and which ones I was going to delegate. It took a major mindset shift for me, but I knew that letting go of so many things that could be done efficiently by others was a crucial next step in my journey.

As Joe and I flew to Austin, Texas for the seminar, he began to tell me about one of his favorite business icons, Elon Musk. Musk's methodology has had an impact on Joe, and also led into the next important step in my coaching.

The CEO began, "My dream car had always been a Tesla. I saw what Elon Musk was doing and I knew I wanted to be part of it by owning an electric car. I ended up buying one a few years ago, one of the first Model X's. It had a function built in called Autopilot. If you turned Autopilot on, the car would stay within the lanes at the same speed and adjust its speed based on vehicles around you."

Joe continued, "There is a freeway in Orange County that I'm sure you are familiar with, Highway 91. I took it often to my office. There were many areas where it has concrete dividers, especially in the carpool lane. The first day I tested the autopilot, I let it drive me the entire way on the freeway by itself. My hands were barely touching the steering wheel. It hugged the concrete divider and kept a distance of maybe one or two feet going 80 miles an hour. It wasn't perfect, so the Tesla would creep closer and closer to the wall and then go back towards the center of the lane. Honestly, it sort of freaked me out. For the first two weeks, I had incredible tension just getting used to the vehicle driving itself at that high speed next to a concrete divider. It took me about 30 days to get used to the autopilot.

"What impressed me most was that Tesla had truly built a machine that could take you where you wanted to go with limited involvement. It was incredible. There were hundreds of pieces that all came together to make this work: sensors, cameras, AI, computer systems, batteries, wheels, motors, electrical connectors, screens, etc. If any one of these fails, it could mean death. However, if they were built well enough, this machine allows the driver to have freedom."

"Skylar, your business is a machine. You are Elon Musk, the designer. Your goal is to design the most efficient, systemized, profitable machine possible. Inside your machine, there are many gears—gears that all operate independently but together. These gears are all of your processes that make up the larger systems. The processes are what run your system. Does that make sense?"

"I think so," I responded.

"Here, open up your guidebook to the next section about the Four Pillar Framework. You see this picture of a gearbox? You can think of your business this way. The entire gearbox is the system/machine. What runs the gearbox is all of the processes—the individual gears. All of your individual processes make your entire system function in unison," Joe explained and instructed me to read further in this section.

As the designer of your machine, your role is to create the "gears" or processes that operate together as one whole machine. The better you get at this, the easier and more efficiently the business will operate. This is a skill you must master. To do so, you will consider four critical pillars to your business.

These four pillars are a part of a business operating system. Every computer has an operating system. This operating system runs the hardware on the computer. Without the operating system, the hardware would not operate correctly. The operating system tells the hardware when and how it should run. It does this over and over, and it does it the same way every time. Businesses also need an operating system. The Four Pillar Framework is a business operating system that keeps the business operating consistently and effectively. There are four main parts that we call pillars.

The Four Pillar Framework

People. How do you find and develop A-players along *and* build a culture that keeps them?

Product. What separates you from the competition? Who is your core customer? What is your X-factor?

Process. How do you simplify your processes and standardize them so they can be easily duplicated for growth?

Plan. What is your vision, and what is your plan to execute that vision? What metrics/numbers will drive these results?

The weekend flew by, and our brains were full of tons of innovative material. The exclusive seminar with this great system builder opened my mind and understanding tremendously. Like The CEO, Keith Cunningham is another great example of someone who builds machines to run at a high level of efficiency with or without him.

When it was over, Joe told me to study and implement the next section in the guidebook before our meeting the following week. After thumbing through the material, I saw that there was a lot to cover in just one week's time.

"Joe, I'm not sure I have the time to get through all of this before our next meeting and still run my company effectively," I told him.

As the words left my lips, I could sense what Joe was about to say. He simply smiled and pointed to one of the core traits of a successful leader in the guidebook: *solutions-focused*.

"Skylar, give me a solution for you not having enough time to get through this larger section before our next meeting."

I realized I still had a long way to go in order to develop into the leader I aspired to be. I threw out the first thought that came to my mind. "I can wake up two and a half hours earlier in the morning, which would be about 4:00 a.m.," I said, hoping for a little recognition of my obvious sacrifice and effort to make it happen. However, Joe did not seem to think that was much of a sacrifice—rather a new standard of excellence.

"Great! Getting up earlier as a new habit will serve you well. I also wake up at 4:00 a.m. I knew you would come up with a viable solution!" Joe complimented.

In an instant, I was blindsided with having just committed to waking up at 4:00 a.m.—and I was the one who came up with it!

Then The CEO had a little mercy on me and grinned. "I do realize it is a lot of material to implement in just one week. How about we reconvene in one month?" Joe suggested.

"That sounds great. I know with waking up earlier I can make it happen," I responded gratefully.

"And remember, just because you now have these projects doesn't mean you can ignore your family. It just means you must be even more intentional with them. I want you to turn off your phone at 5:00 or 6:00 p.m. when you get home, so you can be totally present with them. Can you commit to that?"

"Yes sir," I replied, my fingers already itching for my phone.

Before parting, Joe emphasized that once I was clear on my roles as the CEO, I must get the culture right. He stated intentionally, *"You will have a culture by design or a culture by default. Either way, you will have a culture, so why not design it to be what you want?"*

I was starting to see the bigger picture clearer now, so I wasted no time and dove into the next section *early*–if you know what I mean.

CHAPTER 12

PEOPLE

I picked up my notebook and started to read about the four pillars.

Pillar #1: People.

"How do you find and develop A-players and build a culture that keeps them?"

The quickest way to build an average company with average profits is to hire average team members. Several years ago, I scaled my first company in the debt consolidation industry. While I was learning the business, I met Gerry, the top sales rep at a local competitor. After our first hire didn't work out, I decided to reach out to Gerry. He liked our vision and decided to leave his company to come work for our startup. Gerry ended up being our #1 sales rep on a regular basis and was one of the reasons we were able to hit over $1,000,000 in revenue our first year. He had a work ethic and sales ability that was unmatched. Gerry was our first A-player and gave us a model to hire many more like him.

The faster you find your A-players, the faster you reach the success you want. It makes logical sense: the better people you have, the better your company will be. However, many business owners don't operate this way. They end up hiring whoever will come work for them. And when those people do not work out, they keep them on the team longer than they should.

Think of your business as a professional sports team. You are the coach, and you are responsible for finding the very best players to win the playoffs. Your goal is to find people who have world-class skills and attitudes—people who are committed to winning. Adversely, you are also responsible for removing or coaching any players that don't fit that description.

Make a list of the people on your team right now. If you have a very large team, list the people in the most important roles. Next to each of their names, give them a grade. Are they A-players (best in their class, committed to winning and supporting the company, with a great attitude and skills, and successful in their current role) or would you give them a B or a C?

A-players: High performers, self-motivated, driven, love winning, embrace accountability, and match the company culture.

B-players: Good performers. Sometimes need motivation; in general, they match the culture; do not care for accountability. Or they are great performers but have a poor attitude, or are in it for themselves.

C-players: Average performers. They miss details, always have too much on their plate, do not like being held accountable, always need motivation and pep talks.

Ranking My Current Team

Name of Team Member	Grade: A, B, or C

Did you notice that I didn't mention D or F players? Most companies get rid of their D or F players right away. That's easy. The hardest thing to do is to part with a C or B player who is in a key role. Maybe he or she is your friend from college or a family member. Perhaps they are someone who has been with the company for a long time, and you feel bad about firing them.

By not letting them go, you are hindering the growth and success of the entire company. Also, you are making your life much more difficult than if you had the right people. I can attribute most of the struggles in my company to having B or C-players in important roles. Almost always, when I replaced those team members with A-players, I was amazed at how much more got done. They would not only get more work done, but there would be fewer headaches. Less chaos. B or C-players tend to create chaos around them when they get busy.

My Philosophy Around Letting People Go

Many business owners hold on to people who are not the "right fit" because of two reasons:

- They feel bad about letting the person go.
- They need someone to fill that role and therefore are not willing to let them go yet.

By holding on to people who are not the right fit for your company, you are hurting yourself, your team members, and that specific team member. Look at this a different way, and with a new perspective: the person you are holding onto may be able to produce better results at a different company and therefore have more fulfillment and happiness. By selfishly holding on to that team member for an extended period, you are preventing them from finding their dream job or career. The right thing to do is to let them go and allow them to find a new home where they can thrive. I have found that team members who are not performing well are usually unhappy and/or unsatisfied. The second I know that someone is not the ideal fit, I start the process to either coach them or build a plan to help them move on.

This exercise of identifying my current team with a grade was a huge eye-opener. I saw that I had a handful of A-players, a few B-players, and the rest fell into the C and below categories. I knew I had to implement what The CEO was telling me, as I did not want to catch that ferocious disease of FTI. So, I took action immediately. After evaluating each team member thoroughly and seeking the counsel of my team leaders, we let go of about 25% of our team who clearly did not fit our company culture and performed as a C-player or below. We had already spent a significant amount of time coaching and trying to help these team members change. It was a bold move, but it also caused the existing A and B-players to step up. It also made more room for A-players. I let my team members know where I felt they stood. I decided to give the B-players an opportunity to rise to the occasion, or they, too, would be invited to leave. I was amazed how this literally changed our company culture almost overnight.

What Happens When Your Company Outgrows Your People?

As your company grows, the people who were originally successful will start to show cracks in their skills and abilities. The friend who you hired in the beginning to help you sell is no longer able to keep up with the high volume of customers, or the manager who was good at managing three people can no longer effectively manage the eight people under him. As you grow, many times you will outgrow your team members. This happens in every company. The question is, will you continue to keep those people who are consistently underperforming (even after coaching), or will you replace them with A-players?

This is one of the main reasons I have built a culture of personal and professional growth. I understand that I tend to build high-growth companies, and I want my team members to be able to keep up. They need to keep learning and growing. So, I get them into personal development seminars, management seminars, industry-specific conferences and training, etc. I hire coaches and consultants for my managers. We read books as a team. The more I can help develop my team, the more likely their skills will be able to match the growth of the company.

Inevitably, there will be team members who cannot keep up. Your option at that point would be some coaching and development to see if they can learn the required skills. If they cannot, it may be time to move on.

Putting the Right People in the Right Seats

Can you have the right person (an A-player) but have them still underperform? Yes! They may be in the wrong seat. I see myself as the conductor of the orchestra. I have a wide range of talented individuals who play different instruments. It is my role as the conductor to make sure that the people are playing in the right roles.

More often than not, your best salesperson will not do really well at managing salespeople. The person who is skilled at closing deals does not necessarily have the same ability when it comes to holding people accountable, coaching, and managing them. It takes much more patience. Moving that salesperson to a management role would be putting the right person in the wrong seat. It is our job to identify the strengths and weaknesses of our players to make sure their role best suits them.

At my company, I have an exceptional business development representative. He is a superstar. He's also a cheerleader for the company and really encompasses our core values. On the outside, it seems like he would make an ideal manager for the department. He has the charisma, the experience closing the deals, etc. However, based on past experience, his personality, behaviors, and assessments we've done, we realized that he would not do as well in a management role. They require two different skill sets. You must understand this and be very mindful of the roles people are in.

I use a custom DISC personality assessment to get clarity into someone's personality style. It will tell me if they are more dominant or have more of an analytical personality. It will tell me if they prefer working with people or working alone, etc. I use this assessment to help identify the ideal roles for our team members. The report I use also shows what motivates people and how to put them in the right roles based on their core motivations. Some people are more money-motivated, while others may be motivated by supporting others.

You can learn more about these assessments at:
www.2dayceo.com/resources/DISC

Promote from Within When Possible

Promoting an up-and-coming team member from within does many things. It improves morale and creates longevity when team members know that they have an opportunity to move up within the organization. It is especially effective for management or leadership roles, as those people understand the company at its core. They already understand the company's values and culture. Whenever possible, promote from within.

I considered who in our company could be promoted from within right away to take on a more significant role—especially after I just let 25% of my company go. The person that kept coming to mind was Melissa. Melissa started out as an office assistant (she was the one who found out that Holly, our previous office manager, had been embezzling). Melissa has always had a tenacity and willingness to learn. I noticed as new roles opened up, she naturally pursued them. I decided to move her from office manager to operations manager, having full confidence in her as an A-player. She had some things to learn, but she stepped into the new role like a champion.

Hiring

If people are your most important asset, then finding, hiring, leading, and developing them will be one of your most important skill sets. We have had many failures in hiring. This is probably why we have become so good at it. When I say we, I mean my team and I. They have seen the failures, and we have learned from them together.

Create and Document the Interview Process

What is the ideal interview process? It depends on what your goal is. If your goal is to consistently hire top performers who fit into the company culture and can "own" their role, you need to master the interview process. Here are my best practices. These have been refined over several hundred interviews and hires.

Document your entire hiring process and share it with your managers. It is important that they know the hiring/interview process so they can follow it.

Write out the specific interview questions that you ask on the first, second, and third interviews. It is imperative that you write these questions out and ask them the same way each time. What sometimes happens during an unscripted interview is you can get into deep conversation with the person and end up emotionally liking them, so you neglect to ask the hard questions. That is a recipe for failure that I have experienced *many times*. Even if you like the person, always ask them the hard questions to uncover any potential issues.

Document their answers. It is important to document their answers so you can look back on failed hires to see what was missed or if there were any red flags that you overlooked (and to document your hiring decisions in case of any future conflicts or litigation).

Keep it simple. Use a one-page "scorecard" during the interview process instead of a long job description. There is a great book that goes into this in detail: *Who: The Method of Hiring*, by Geoff Smart. This one-page scorecard has the mission and three to five specific outcomes for the position, and the skills needed for the role. It uses an ongoing A/B/C grading chart next to the outcomes to see how you rate the person during the interview process, once they are hired, and how they are doing each year.

You can get a free copy of one here::
www.2dayceo.com/resources

Involve Others

Involve key leaders and other managers in the interview process. It is always more effective to have different perspectives from your team members and get their feedback. They will also be working with this person, so it is important to involve them in the process.

Assess Applicants Using your Core Values

If your goal is to build a culture that represents your core values, always assess your candidates based on how well they do that. We do this by asking well-thought-out questions for each core value. It is important that you do not ask the candidate what they think of the core value or if they "are" the core value. For example, don't ask "Do you have integrity?" or "Do you have an "own it" mentality?" The candidates will obviously always say the right things to get the job. The questions must be carefully crafted to give you insight into the way the candidate thinks and operates. "Can you share a time with me when you demonstrated integrity in your life?" or "Tell me about a time when your boss reprimanded you but you believed you did nothing wrong." In that question, we would be asking to find out how much of an "own it" mentality they have.

Speak 80/20

What I've noticed during interviews with CEOs I have coached is that they talk too much during the interview. Why is the interviewer talking more than the candidate? The goal is to get the candidate talking 80% of the time while you talk 20% of the time, mainly through questioning. You want to ask questions during the entire interview to see how they respond.

I put together a video to show you how to properly interview at:
www.2dayceo.com/resources

Always Be in the Alpha Position

Remember, the interviewee is coming to interview at your company. Make sure you show up that way. Many people oversell their company, which puts them in a beta position. Remember, your company is awesome. They are coming to work for a company that really cares and invests in their team members. Maintain control, and the alpha position, by asking the questions. Whoever is asking the questions is typically in control of the conversation.

Ask the Hard Questions

One of my favorite interview questions is, "What wouldn't you want me to know about you?" This question uncovers some interesting things. Remember, your goal is to dive as deep as legally possible to get to know this person—for their benefit as well as yours. You want to make sure the team member will be happy at your company. It needs to be a win/win.

(I've written down my favorite interview questions, including the juicy ones. You can get them at http://www.2dayceo.com/resources/tools/interview-questions)

A Structured Interview Process

First Interview

This can be done on the phone or in person. I usually make an initial call to "feel out" the candidate. You can often learn about a person's personality, ambition, intelligence, etc. over the phone. If they seem like a good fit, I will invite them to a second in-person interview.

Personality Assessment

Have the candidate complete a personality assessment. I use a custom DISC assessment tool which I linked to in the previous section. These reports give you great insights into the team member's personality, work style, motivators, etc. I can tell immediately what role this person would be ideal for based on the results of the profile.

Second Interview: In-person Culture Interview

This interview will be more focused on seeing if the candidate is a cultural fit. We ask many questions related to the company's core values, the person's personal interests and attitudes, etc. We want to know if we would want to hang out with this person outside of work or not. We ask a few questions about their skills and experience but keep the focus on culture. As the CEO, if you have not mastered the interview process and the questions, I would do as many of these yourself as possible. Also, whenever you get the opportunity, bring some of your other managers into the interview so they can see the process.

Third Interview: In-person Skill Interview

This interview dives deep into the skills and abilities related to the role they are interviewing for. It is important to get different perspectives during the interview process, so I usually have the direct supervisor for the role do the third interview. They have more insight into what specific skills are required for the position.

Fourth and Additional Interviews

We take as much time as needed to make sure the person is the right fit. Sometimes we do four, five, or even six interviews if we are not sure. If you are not 90%+ sure they are the right fit for the company, do not hire them. I repeat, do not hire them. Wait for the right A-player. They may be one candidate away.

Lunch/Dinner Meeting (Optional)

I gained this insight from Dave Ramsey's book, Entre-Leadership. For any management, upper management, or key roles, we take the candidate and their spouse out for dinner as the final "get to know you" opportunity. We let them know that we have a family feel, and it's important for their spouse to get to know us also. Most candidates have never experienced anything like this before, and it really drives home how great of a company and culture you have. It also gets their spouse to buy in to the company, which is extremely important. You don't want a key team member's spouse complaining each day about why they work so much. Use this time to build a relationship with the spouse. You may be surprised at what information the spouse ends up sharing.

Benefits of an In-Depth Interview Process

- You have a better chance of identifying who is and who is not an A-player.

- The more you meet with the candidate, the more comfortable they become, and the more you truly get to know the person. You do not really get to see the true sides of people until the third or fourth meeting.

- The longer the interview process, the more likely the team member will remain a part of your organization long-term. The more hoops a candidate has to jump through, the more committed they are to the process. If they have one quick 15-minute interview, they have less to lose by quitting after a week due to a better job offer. However, if they spent two weeks interviewing with you, they have already invested too much time to think twice about an offer from another company.

Hire Slow, Fire Fast

This seems to be a rule that all CEOs know, but for whatever reason have a hard time following. Here is the typical scenario: Johnny has been on your team for two years. He is a pretty good team member, but not incredible. He is average, you might say. The team really likes Johnny because he is very friendly. Johnny's performance starts dropping, and he is not helping the business in a big way. You don't want to fire Johnny because the team likes him, and you don't know who would do all his work. So, you start to put some pressure on Johnny to do a better job. Johnny starts to get defensive now that his poor performance is being pointed out, and he starts to become negative. You know you should fire Johnny, but it's hard. He's been a decent team member for a while.

So, you let time pass: one month, three months, six months... performance does not improve. Twelve months go by like this before you finally fire Johnny. To your surprise, your team actually feels better with Johnny gone. Your company ends up running fine without Johnny, and you notice your culture improves. You end up hiring an A-player to replace him, and to your surprise, Johnny didn't handle that much work and was very replaceable. You ask yourself, "Why did I wait so long to fire Johnny?"

This happens time and time again, even with the most experienced CEOs and managers. You get comfortable with your current team members and don't let go of the low performers. This does more damage than you know. What you do not realize is that Johnny is taking the A-player's seat. The A-player is out there in the marketplace looking for a company like yours. Your fear is that you will not be able to find a better replacement than Johnny. *There is always a better replacement* for B and C performers. You must trust this.

What is the cost of keeping team members who are poor performers or cultural misfits?

- Your team morale drops. Top performers want to be around other top performers.

- You aren't able to hire that A-player who is currently looking for that role.

- You may lose key team members or managers who are having to do more work because of the poor performer.

- Your company does not reach its revenue or profit targets.

Onboarding

"You're hired!"

"Great, when do I start?"

"Right now."

"But I haven't had any training!"

"Oh, you can learn on the job. Grab a hammer!"

That's how many people's onboarding experiences go. It is imperative that you stay disciplined in onboarding team members properly. Their careers depend on it.

A couple of years into our business I hired a technician. Our process had been to have the new team member "shadow" for a couple of days. Well, it was his first day, and I ended up getting a call to a job a couple of hours away. I brought him with me and ended up getting the job. We didn't have anyone to do it, so I gave him a hammer and some tools to remove some glue-down wood flooring and left him to go lock in another job. I picked him up later that night. He had struggled to do the job properly and was very upset. The floor was a mess. Do not do this. This is a poor way to onboard and train new team members.

Having an efficient and effective onboarding process is important to help new team members integrate and learn their roles. Yes, you can just throw them on the job. However, that is not the best way to show your new team member that you run a tight ship.

Start by creating a simple onboarding plan that includes the following:

- Integration into culture. Share your core values and some background on your company: how you got started, etc. Help connect the new team member to the vision of the company.

- Connect them to the team. Assign someone to take the new team member out to lunch (ideally one of your top company cheerleaders). Introduce them to as many other team members as possible during their first week.

Create a training plan and share it with the new team member. For instance, "Spend one day with John, one day with Mike, go to five jobs on your third day, watch three presentations…"

Create a checklist for them and follow up on it.

Check out the onboarding checklist we use at www.2dayceo.com/resources/tools/onboarding

I spent some time reviewing our hiring process. I realized that most of our bad hires were due to a poor and unintentional process. Our old interview process looked like this: we would post an ad online for a position. We would bring in a candidate for one interview. If we liked them, we would hire them within the next day or two. Then they would start and we would throw them into a truck to shadow someone until we felt they were ready to do the job on their own. This proved to be very ineffective.

So, we went to work and developed the process modeled above. We wrote down set interview questions for each role, made a scorecard for each role, and then did a three-step interview process with assessments. We experienced immediate improvement in bringing in quality hires and training them well. I knew this would be the path to get our A-team in place so I could eventually get my business running on its own.

Developing Your Leadership Team

A final concern of the People pillar is your leadership team. It is never too early to start building your leadership team—unless you don't have any team members. If you have team members, you can start involving those people in the decisions that move the company towards its goals. There are incredible benefits to involving people within your organization in a leadership team—sometimes referred to as a management team.

My first leadership team was made up of an estimator, a salesperson, our office manager, and our bookkeeper. We set up a weekly meeting that discussed the hot topics of the company and how we would handle them. This team was critical in gathering the different perspectives to propel the company forward. They were responsible for some of the main initiatives that help refine our culture and processes. The people on this team started to feel like they were truly valued and transitioned from a team member mindset to more of an ownership mindset. They started to care more about how their decisions affected the entire company.

How to Set Up an Effective Leadership Team and Meeting Structure

Choose three to six of your top leaders within the organization. These are department heads or influencers. Select a person from each area of the company so you can get different perspectives. If you have a small team, it's okay to have two people from the same department. If you have a larger company, you will want to have your leadership team composed of executives/upper management.

Set a day and time each week to have a weekly one-hour meeting. This meeting is mandatory and cannot be missed.

Communicate to your new leadership team that it is a privilege to be on this team. If at any moment they feel like it's a drag, we will get someone else to sit in their seat.

Create a Leadership Meeting Agenda. Ours has the following:

- Everyone shares wins from last week.

- Review core values (until they are ingrained into your team).

- Review key metrics/KPIs.

- Discuss what is working and what is not working. Have each member come prepared with this. This is the most important part of the meeting, as this provides the chance to start making progress on areas of the business that aren't working.

It is important that you create a culture of trust, respect, and truthfulness within the leadership team. They will be responsible for having hard conversations and bringing up issues that are currently preventing the company from achieving its goals. Once these hot topics are brought up, it is important to discuss them without the fluff. What is the real issue and what do we need to do to resolve it? In these leadership meetings, you should be able to discuss almost anything, including team member issues, culture issues, processes breaking down, compliance issues, etc. Allow your team members to come up with the solutions. Do not try and solve everything for them. You want this team to eventually be running the company and making most decisions on their own.

To build a culture of trust within the team, you must also be open and honest as the CEO. Share what you are feeling. Be vulnerable. Talk about the issues of the business. The more you share the challenges you are having, the more the team will start to open up and trust each other. You will only know you went too far when you go too far. Then just reign it back a little. Most leaders never go too far; they typically carry a facade and act like they always have it together.

Conflict. It is important to have healthy conflict within these meetings. If a team member disagrees with something or someone, they must speak up about it. If they are not speaking up, there is usually a lack of trust. Conflict is healthy. Conflict is very important to help companies progress. The type of conflict that is not healthy is the type that involves attacks and disrespect—that is not okay. *You and your team must learn to embrace healthy and productive conflict.* Addressing conflict head-on was one of my leadership weaknesses for much of my career. It was the reason for high turnover, resentment, and unresolved issues.

I pulled together my key people from each department and launched this practice of a weekly leadership meeting. I did not hold back, and I shared with them that I had some trust issues as an owner. Due to the fact that we had a team member embezzle company funds years before, and also because a team member recently stole our largest account, I sometimes had trouble trusting the team. I told them I did not want this to be the case. I wanted them to fully trust me, and I wanted to fully trust them. This was a very awkward and hard conversation at first, but it ended up being a healing conversation for everyone. Our team was noticeably stronger and committed because of that direct conversation, and another important aspect of our new culture had been established.

I could tell I was changing as a leader, but I was physically exhausted nearly every day, and my energy was up and down constantly. My patience was short far too often, both at the office and at home, and sadly, I was not bringing the same energy home that I seemed to be applying at work. While my business seemed to be progressing well, my body felt like it was on an uncontrollable downward spiral.

Review and Evaluations of Lessons Learned

Circle your current, honest answer.
1 = Not true at All and 5 = Completely true

My team is mostly made up of A and B-players.

1   2   3   4   5

I have a structured hiring process that is followed for every hire.

1   2   3   4   5

I regularly focus on developing leaders within my company.

1   2   3   4   5

For any answer that is not a 5,
what specific actions can you take to improve? ?

_____

_____

_____

_____

CHAPTER 13

PRODUCT

I labored diligently to put my new People processes in place, as I wanted to have strong forward momentum before I met with The CEO again. I also knew that I was laying a solid foundation, and the structure on top of that foundation would be constructed over time. Everything Joe was teaching me, both in person and from his guidebook, was proving to be worth its weight in gold.

My next meeting had arrived, and I sat in Joe's conference room drinking one of my daily bottles of soda. I was ready to learn the next important pillar of his business system, but Joe unexpectedly paused and glanced at what I was drinking.

"How long have you been drinking that unhealthy stuff, Skylar?"

"Umm, off and on for the last few years, but a lot more lately," I confessed.

"When you say, 'a lot more lately,' what do you mean specifically?" Joe pressed.

Finding no way around it, I admitted, "I drink two or three bottles a day, and sometimes more."

"Why would you do that to yourself?" Joe asked.

His response served as a simple yet sharp rebuke of a health habit I knew was not serving a positive purpose in my life. I could sense we were about to talk about something other than business because Joe pulled up a chair next to me and sat down. He folded his arms and leaned back in his chair, contemplating his next words. I sat in silence, a little nervous about the direction of our conversation.

The subsequent questions felt like an interrogation. "Skylar, have you been waking up early at 4:00 a.m., like you said you were going to?"

"Yes sir, and that is why I think I have been drinking more soda, to keep my energy going," I responded, hoping it would serve as some sort of validation.

"And how is that formula working for you?" Joe asked.

"That formula?" I asked seeking clarification.

"Yes, the formula of drinking sugar, caffeine, and chemicals to keep your body going. Are you working out in the mornings?"

There was no escaping it. I had not worked out in who knows how long, and I am pretty sure Joe already knew it. Nonetheless, I answered his question. "I haven't been working out because I figured I should be spending all of my time implementing what you have been teaching me."

"Well, I'll take some of the responsibility, then. I should have been clearer in the beginning of our coaching agreement. You must make fitness and healthy living a daily part of your life if you are going to truly rise up to your God-given potential," Joe instructed.

"I know, Joe. It's not your responsibility. I'm aware I've let my health and fitness slip, thinking it was justified for some reason. But the fact is, while I am grateful my business is going well, I feel drained and spent at the end of the day, and too often my family gets the brunt of it. The measly leftovers from the feast, the crumbs of the dessert, the . . ." But before I could continue my pitiful admission, Joe interjected.

"Look here, Skylar," Joe said, peering into my eyes with a raised tone that was inescapable. "I don't care how tired you are, how mentally spent you are from work, or even if you experienced something unfavorable in business that day and you feel completely empty. When you get home, *there is always more fuel in the tank for your family!* And not just any fuel—the best and highest quality fuel. The premium grade. Do you understand?"

The CEO's rebuke struck my heart to the core, and tears filled my eyes as I bowed my head to hide my emotions. Joe stood up and got some tissues for me from the corner of the conference room. Then he sat by me again, put his hand on my shoulder, and continued in a softer tone.

"Skylar, your family deserves your best. Always! Too often, people—especially men—forget that their most important appointment and deal of the day is the one within the walls of their own home. It is a mental part of our fitness. We must be strong mentally just as much as physically. If you commit to working out daily and get your blood flowing, it will make a huge impact on your ability to give your best at home as well." He paused, and then lowered the boom on my soda habit. "Also—referring to your personal tank—only take in things that will benefit you at the highest level. You wouldn't consciously put bleach in your car's oil tank just because you thought it was similar, would you? That would be ludicrous and detrimental to your vehicle. Only put things in your personal tank that are advantageous. That includes food and drink but includes other things as well."

"Yes sir," I humbly agreed, and realized I had just committed to working out consistently.

I excused myself to the restroom to gather my emotions. I splashed some water on my face, then looked at myself in the mirror. I repeated to myself aloud, *"Skylar, there is always more room in your tank for your family.* From this day forward, my family will get my best when I am home!"

As I returned to the conference room, I felt a new resolve to take the fitness aspect of my life more seriously. Joe was mapping out some things on the whiteboard. I went straight over and grabbed the soda on the conference table and threw it in the garbage can. Joe started clapping in recognition of my decision.

"Well done, Skylar, well done. Are you ready to move forward with the next business pillar now?" Joe asked.

"Yes sir, let's do it!" I answered energetically.

He brought up the fact that we were obviously in the same industry, but bluntly asked, "Skylar, why do you think my company's revenue is well into eight figures and yours is still in the low seven?"

I had a few different ideas, but the one I decided to say was, "You've just been in business a lot longer than me and have figured out some things that myself and others have not," I said hoping it would suffice.

"I can appreciate that answer, but there is definitely a lot more to it," Joe stated with conviction. "All of my businesses are successful across three completely different industries for a specific reason," Joe said.

Not waiting around for the answer, I prodded, "And what is that reason, Joe?"

"Because we provide more value than anyone else in that industry," Joe responded.

It was a loaded question with a loaded answer, and Joe said I would discover what all of that meant as I read and implemented the next section in his guidebook, Product. It had four steps of explanation and action. Joe gave me another month to put the foundation in place, and I went straight to work on it.

Step 1. Know Your X-Factor

You can have the right people, but if your product is not exceptional, you will struggle. If you are in the service industry, your product is the service you offer to customers. The question you should always be asking yourself is, *"How can I provide more value than anyone else for my customers?"* That is a winning question that will lead you to the right answers.

Business is all about creating value for your customers. Whoever creates the most value has the most customers and gets the opportunity to charge the most. Think of the brands that went from nothing to mega-successful companies: Tesla, Apple, Amazon, Netflix, etc. If you have done business with any of these brands, you know that they are all about providing as much value as possible through their product, service, or both.

When I first bought my Tesla, I was able to customize my vehicle and place the final order online. This took so much of the headache away. I did not have to deal with a sales rep, negotiations, etc. Amazon decided to do two-day delivery when their competition was offering five- and seven-day delivery times, and they did it for free! *Provide more value than anyone else in your industry.*

Netflix originally became popular when it decided it would mail DVDs to customers' houses instead of making them go to a retail location. They went a step further and gave you the option to put the old one back in the envelope and mail it back. You never had to leave your house! Then they went even further by giving you unlimited rentals. *Provide more value than anyone else in your industry.* There are thousands of other examples of companies that focus on providing more value than anyone else.

Finding the answer to this question takes time. It takes *thinking time* – time you dedicate solely to just thinking. Strategizing. Planning. If you want to produce big results, you must be strategic. I dedicate anywhere from one to two distraction-free hours each week just for thinking.

The biggest mistake most organizations make is that they fall in love with their business or products instead of what their client wants. What does your client want? Have you asked? Have you personally reached out to a group of customers and asked what they want from your company and what would really amaze them?

You must find a way to provide more value than anyone else. Value what your customer wants, not what you think is valuable. This will be your X-factor.

Take a moment and answer these three questions to gain insight into how you can provide more value than anyone else.

1. What are your customers' pain points?

_____

_____

_____

_____

_____

_____

_____

_____

2. Where do your customers get let down by the competition?

_____

_____

_____

_____

_____

_____

3. Where can you provide more value to your customer?

_____

_____

_____

_____

_____

_____

_____

Who Is Your Core Customer—Otherwise Known as an Avatar?

Most smaller companies try to throw a very large net and capture as many customers as possible. However, the quickest way to grow is to find your ideal customer and structure your product for them. Identify their pain points, struggles, and buying styles, and then develop your entire product/service to meet their needs. Sure, your product may appeal to others, but you must get clear on who will primarily be buying your product or using your service so you can specifically target and satisfy them.

Start with identifying who is most likely to buy your product:

- What gender?
- What age bracket?
- What income range?
- What geographic location?
- How do they communicate? (email, text, social media, phone, etc.)
- How do they like to buy? (Do they prefer to buy in-person? Over the phone or internet?)
- What are the biggest pains/struggles that your product will solve for them?

Describe your core customer.

_____

_____

_____

_____

I have created a document to help you gain clarity around your core customer/avatar. You can get it here: www.2dayceo.com/resources

Step 2. Create Your Brand Promise

What are you *specifically* known for in your customers' minds? A brand promise is what your brand will represent in its marketing, and what you will be known for.

Here are some examples of well-known brand promises:

- Geico: 15 minutes or less can save you 15% or more on car insurance.

- BMW: The ultimate driving machine.

- Apple: Think Different.

- Walmart: Save Money, Live Better.

These brand promises were well thought out. First, the company identified who their core customer was and what they want to be known for. Then they put together a clear and simple statement that could be reiterated in all their marketing and communication.

What is the simple, clear brand promise your business makes to its customers?

_____

_____

Step 3. Provide more value than anyone else

The new standard in service is getting everything right. If you communicate on time, provide the product/service that you said you were going to, and then make the experience good, you pass. Just because you did everything you said you were going to do when you said you were going to do it does not mean that you are providing more value than others. That is now the standard in service. So, the question is, what are you doing to provide MORE VALUE than anyone else in your industry?

One of Amazon's many claims to fame was when it decided to do two-day shipping. Years ago, shipping took 5 to 7 business days. If you wanted something shipped faster, you would pay a very hefty price. So, everyone just got used to 5-to-7-day shipping. Amazon knew that the more value they provided, the more customers they would gain. That's how it is in every industry. So, they decided that they would offer FREE 2-day shipping for millions of Amazon Prime subscribers. This was unheard of. I remember when they launched this, I went out of my way to introduce Amazon to as many people as I could. I became a brand ambassador. They provided more value than anyone else in the industry. This is just one of the many ways Amazon provides more value than most of its competitors.

The question you should constantly be asking yourself and your team is, "How do we provide more value than anyone else?" At one of our experiential events that we put on, we go above and beyond in almost every way to blow our attendees' minds. They think they are just coming to a business seminar. Most business seminars are very boring. Attendees sit in their seats for 8+ hours listening to a speaker. We changed that. We start off the experience by loading the attendees into a brand-new Sprinter van, blindfolded. We then do 10+ world-class experiences outside of the classroom throughout this 3-day event. Each day we add more and more value through experiences and through high quality gifting. We give out water bottles, shirts, backpacks, notebooks, quality pens, graduation gifts, etc. We do all of this to provide more value than anyone else.

Zappos became famous because it became the only company that would allow you to return new shoes that you purchased through them with no questions asked. You could buy 15 pairs of shoes and then return all of them. This was not the normal way that online retail did business 10+ years ago. However, this was valuable to customers. So, people kept coming back and referring everyone they knew to Zappos. They eventually became known for having one of the best customer experiences for an online retailer.

What can you do to provide more value than anyone in your industry? It could be a better experience for your customers. A thoughtful note. Better communication. Better quality products. Faster shipping. Additional product offerings. A guarantee. The list is endless. The point is, you must sit down and strategically think about what you can do to provide more value. The answers will come. However, it requires intentional thought.

An exercise I regularly do is to ask what the pain points are for people who purchase from us or competitors. If you can figure out a solution to an industry's prevalent pain point/challenge, you win. This is what Amazon did. This is what Zappos did.

What are some ideas on ways to provide more value to your clients?

_____

_____

_____

_____

_____

_____

_____

Step 4. Document and Design your Customer Journey

When I coach clients on how to improve their product or service, often they only think of the product they offer—nothing before or after. However, this is only a small part of the complete customer journey. A carpet-cleaning company may spend most of its time thinking about how to clean carpets better. A car dealership may only strategize about how to sell more cars. A CPA may only focus on how to do their client's taxes with a better tax strategy.

The complete customer journey is what happens from the moment the customer hears about you, through their purchase, and including what occurs afterward. In order for a company to thrive and provide the most value through each step, it must put energy and focus on the *entire* customer journey. Wowing the customer at the beginning of their journey is great. However, you want to also WOW them through the entire journey all the way to the end.

I was recently building out a coaching program, and I wanted to create an exceptional experience through the entire customer journey. So, I mapped out the entire process from A-Z on a whiteboard: marketing, the sales call, the investment, the onboarding process, the fulfillment of the coaching, the follow-up process. This intention and practice helped reveal ways we could make every step of the journey incredible.

Let me give you an example. As part of one of my companies, I provide a live seminar experience. When someone signs up for it, they don't just get a welcome email. We mail them a box with high-quality goodies in it. Then we add them to a sequence of emails to provide value before the event. The client then gets access to a series of videos to watch *before* the event so they can get the most from the experience.

At the event, we give them eight different gifts throughout the experience. These are all strategically thought out. When they complete the event, we have a 12-month sequence of mailing them books, mugs, letters, etc. As a result, we regularly get feedback that this was the most incredible event they have ever been a part of. We know this consistent feedback is not a fluke. It is the outcome of all the intentional effort we do before, during, and after to create this exceptional experience.

Some Steps To Help Create Exceptional Customer Experience

- Your current customers will tell you for free what to improve. Survey customers on what part of the process they were least happy with. Ask for feedback on what could have been done better.

- Map out the entire customer journey. Every step. (Visiting your website, the first call, etc.)

- Identify which areas of the customer experience are the most "painful," or have the most friction for your customer.

- Put together a plan to improve your customer's journey. How can you do something different to remove friction and add value?

- Brainstorm all the areas of your customer journey where you can provide more value than your competitors.

As I reflected on our current customer journey, I realized I had never devoted time to think of ways to provide more value than anyone else. Over the next few weeks, I gathered my team leaders, and we executed the steps Joe provided in his guidebook. We decided our new brand promise at Superior Restoration would be, appropriately enough, *Exceptional Experience.*

As we got surveys back from our patrons on what we could do better, we noticed that they regularly mentioned the lack of communication during the construction process. In order to improve their customer journey, we put together a plan to "over-communicate" with customers through text, email, and calls. We began to provide them with better and more communication than any other restoration company.

Also, to provide more value than anyone else, we decided to give gifts to customers towards the end of the construction process. Many customers get impatient when the job is getting close to completion. So, we decided to give them special gifts to show that we cared, and we were doing everything possible to complete the job in a timely manner. We continued to identify other pain points in our process and put together actionable ideas to improve them.

Over time, and with some conscious and consistent effort, our new mission became to *provide more value than anyone else in our industry.* We wanted to create raving fans and took the necessary steps to make that goal a reality. We wanted our customers to go out of their way to refer us to others.

This created a new element in our culture as well. One of our managers presented an idea in one of our team meetings: how could we create an exceptional experience for our own team members and loyal vendors? We recognized that in any organization, there are both internal customers and external customers, and we needed to make sure ALL were receiving an Exceptional Experience! So, we applied the steps to our internal customers as well.

New and expanded team.

REVIEW AND EVALUATIONS OF LESSONS LEARNED

Circle your current, honest answer.
1 = Not true at all and 5 = Completely true

Our X-factor sets us apart from all competition.
(If not, you need a new one.)

1	2	3	4	5

We are clear on our brand promise and regularly utilize it.

1	2	3	4	5

We have raving fans because of the value we provide to our customers.

1	2	3	4	5

I have a clear and documented customer journey.

1	2	3	4	5

For any answer that is not a 5,
what specific actions can you take to improve?

_____

_____

_____

_____

_____

_____

_____

_____

_____

_____

_____

CHAPTER 14

PROCESS

"You seem happier and calmer after work," Jessica observed, after I'd spent a few months implementing Joe's framework of People & Product. I was bringing home my best energy and taking care of my body and health with a higher level of consciousness. "I'm not sure what he's telling you, but just keep doing it, because I already recognize a difference in you being more present at home," she continued.

"I'm glad you noticed and said something, because I'm doing my best to put everything into place as soon as possible, and I've been working out— which you know has made a huge difference in my mental clarity. Are the boys already asleep?" I inquired as I stood and headed towards their bedroom.

"Yes they are, Skylar, so please don't wake them up," Jessica requested.

Our two boys were growing every day. I had been missing the opportunity to just hold them, so I went to where our youngest was sleeping and gently picked him up out of his crib. I sat with him in the rocking chair while he was sound asleep. In a hushed tone, I began to promise him that I was going to do everything possible so Daddy could be home more often. I closed my eyes and began to visualize what that would look like. Jessica slipped quietly into the doorway and observed me. I smiled at her, and although it was dark in the bedroom, the hallway light reflected the happy tears in her eyes. No words needed to be spoken. I knew why she was emotional, and I was determined to create more moments just like this one.

Joe called me early the next morning before our next meeting and said he wanted me to take another few weeks to continue acting on all the principles I had learned. Although I had done everything possible to implement them quickly, it was a delightful surprise to have some more time.

I had shared my business coaching with one of my managers. He approached me and asked how things were coming along. He said that everyone he had talked to in our company seemed to notice a tangible shift in the culture, and the new standard proved to be making a positive difference. Team members were stepping up and filling the gaps of those who were let go. Others expressed they felt more trusted and empowered as I delegated some of my own responsibilities to them.

Up to that point, my every intention and efforts were to sell the company, but maybe something shifted in me as well, because I felt renewed and excited to be the CEO of this company again. Gradually, an unexpected feeling bubbled up inside of me: *I did not want to sell the company anymore, rather I felt a renewed determination to scale it to another level!* I wanted to see what I was capable of building.

The next few weeks passed quickly, and once again I found myself in Joe's conference room, ready for my next instructions. I told him I'd decided to keep my company and not sell, which intrigued him.

"What has changed, Skylar, that you now want to keep your company?" Joe asked.

"Of course, all the things you've been teaching me in person and through your guidebook, but the biggest change has been myself. I'm seeing things through a new set of lenses, and my perspective has broadened," I answered.

Joe was satisfied with my answer. He nodded his head and smiled, saying, "Maybe you treating your body better health and fitness-wise has also contributed to your mental clarity? I notice your energy looks and feels a lot more in harmony with that of a truly successful person."

"Yes sir. I have gone through a bit of a detox physically, and I'm feeling much better now. Thanks again for your help in getting me in shape in all aspects of my life," I said sincerely.

Joe nodded his head, acknowledging my gratitude, then opened his guidebook so we could move forward.

"Skylar, always remember that your systems will set you free! We've talked about the *people* part of your business—the ones who run your system. When you have the *right people*, it will make it easier to run your system. We've also talked about making your product and service exceptional for the customer. Now it's time to discuss designing your system—also known as your *process*. You are the designer of the machine. Your role is to create and tweak the system on a regular basis to help it run more efficiently and effectively. You want to remove or prevent the friction and breakdowns that happen. The simpler you can make the processes within your system, the better," Joe explained.

The CEO pointed out that he'd shared the first part of this section, *Simplify to Scale*, with me a few years ago when Jessica and I were running Lewis Marketing Corp. However, he strongly encouraged me to review it to ensure I was implementing it to its fullest extent. He then instructed me to read through and act on the next portion before our next meeting.

(See Chapter 7 to review the Simplify to Scale section.)

Be Process-driven

To build a machine that can run independently of you, regardless of the retention of the people within your company, is to make it process-driven. You can either have a people-driven company or a process-driven company. People miss details. They are emotional. They can get lazy and unfocused. A process-driven company allows your business to run smoothly, even with people turning some of the levers. It also allows the company to continue to run when key team members leave or are terminated.

There have been multiple times in my businesses when losing a key team member pushed us into crisis mode. After these experiences, I got better and more intentional at building a business that was process-driven instead of people-driven. Don't get me wrong—it still hurts to lose a key team member. However, if they get in an accident or are no longer able to work for us, we will not go under. Being people-driven is risky and ends up consuming more time than just building out the processes the right way.

Review and Document Important Processes

Why would you want to take the time to review and refine your processes and then document them?

Because you are dealing with *people*. These people are all responsible for certain tasks and executing specific processes. Over the course of your business, you may have many team members fill a specific role. If you don't document the processes, you will have to train each new person. As each person trains a new team member, and then they train another team member, the process starts to break down. When that process breaks down, it can cause the machine to operate inefficiently and eventually break down completely. Then you, as the owner, must step in to fix it. That is where many owners spend their time: fixing broken processes that were never properly built, refined, and documented.

Do you need to review and document your processes? Only if you want a business that can operate and grow without you. If you want to be the one putting out fires and regularly fixing things, you do not need to review or document those processes.

Documenting your processes does several things:

- Helps you see where there may be weak links within your process to improve.

- Allows you to duplicate that process more effectively.

- Helps you to train new team members on that process.

- Is a guide for current team members to utilize the process correctly.

What is an SOP?

A Standard Operating Procedure is a written or recorded step-by-step instruction that describes how to perform a specific process within your organization. More organizations use video to document their processes.

Let's say you are in the restaurant business. A restaurant business may have 30 to 100 processes to document. Let's start with the customer intake process. Call it the *Customer Intake SOP*.

- The customer walks in the front door.
- They are greeted and asked if they have a reservation.
- Their presence is noted somewhere on paper or in a piece of software.
- They are invited to have a seat and wait for the next table.

That is as simple as a process gets. There are many more in-depth processes, like opening the restaurant, closing the restaurant, how to make specific dishes, fixing equipment, marketing the business, etc.

Let's create a very basic SOP checklist for opening the restaurant.

- Unlock the door and turn off the alarm
- Walk over to the oven and turn it on to pre-heat
- Verify you have the correct inventory for that day (this should be done the previous day or week)
- Turn on computer systems
- Turn on lights
- Start heating soup
- Start cooking bread
- Prepare tables
- Stock the proper number of menus, utensils and buzzers at the front desk
- Turn on digital "We're Open" sign

By documenting this, you will start to notice areas that can be automated. What if you have the open sign on a timer? You will find ways to create more efficiency through documenting your business processes. Equally as important is having this SOP/checklist so that a new team member knows what to do if the team member assigned to open the restaurant does not show up for work or unexpectedly quits. You *must* have the processes documented in this situation—unless you, as the CEO, want to come in and open it yourself.

A few tips for creating effective SOPs

Start with the most important SOPs. Customer intake, sales process, production process, accounting processes, etc. Avoid overwhelming yourself by attempting to document every process in your company. Set a timeline—perhaps it takes you six months to get through all of them.

Keep them simple. Avoid making them too long or too detailed.

Use videos or images when possible. If you are documenting how to input a customer into your software, use screen capture software to record the whole thing. If you need to document your sales presentation, just record it.

Everyone must follow the processes

Communicate the *why*. Before you reprimand or fire anyone because they consistently ignore the processes, make sure you have communicated *why* they need to follow them.

Let them know that your goal is to have a process-run company, which will make everyone's job easier. They will be able to take time off without coming back to a massive amount of work and issues. The company will run smoothly and more efficiently by following the processes.

No deviation!

If someone is deviating from your written and clearly communicated process, these are the common reasons:

- They are lazy. (Good luck fixing this. You can either let them go or make the process even simpler so they can't mess it up)

- They are rebellious and are purposely not following directions. (Coach them. If there is habitual resistance, remove them from the organization)

- The processes are inefficient or overcomplicated and need to be redone. (Review and adjust the SOP)

If you have a team member who knows the process but just chooses not to do it, this is an issue. Their lethargy is contagious to other team members who are watching them. "If John doesn't follow it, maybe I don't have to either." You want to build a culture where everyone is following the processes and understands why. Sit down with them and ask them why they aren't following the process. Maybe there is a part of the process that does not make sense to them. Maybe there is something they think should not be a part of the SOP. In this case, review the SOP and be open to seeing if there is a better way to do something. If there is, change the SOP.

If they understand the process, have no issues with it, and still choose not to follow it, it may be time to move on from that team member.

CEOs/Managers must *lead by example*

At one point, we kept running into an issue with our team members not submitting their receipts. They would purchase work-related materials, supplies, etc. for the company, but forget to give the receipts to our accounting manager. So, we had a simple Google form created that allowed all our team members to submit receipts on their phone, at the time of purchase, instead of waiting until the end of the week. This was a much more efficient process and immediately improved the number of receipts we received.

Initially, I just wanted to stick with the way I had always done it because it was easier for me. However, I knew that as the leader, I needed to follow the same process as everyone else.

You are not above following the processes. If you don't adhere to them, you will be a roadblock to the change that you are striving to make within your company.

Institutional Knowledge

The people who control the knowledge become the lifeblood of the organization. The last thing you want is one person within your organization who has all the knowledge necessary to run the business. If you lose this person, you could potentially lose your business as well. The way around this is to build a process-driven organization that does not rely on one individual's knowledge. The knowledge inside each person's head must be pulled out and well documented. As long as it is documented, you can find a skilled candidate who can follow the steps within the process.

You must get the knowledge out of your people's heads. You may get some resistance from some of your higher-level team members, as they may believe that if they don't "own" that knowledge, they become less valuable. So, they hoard the knowledge. They do not share it with anyone else, and that prevents other people from becoming as good as them.

Recognize the people who possess this knowledge and help them understand that they will be more valuable if they share their knowledge and help build people up. If they are not willing to open up, they are too big a risk for your company. This could be a salesperson who knows how to sell to a particular industry, or a software developer who is the only one who knows how to decipher the code. Don't tolerate this. Start building a culture of openness and transparency.

Utilizing Technology

While there are some processes that require a human being to complete them, most can benefit from utilizing technology/software/machines to systemize the business. This often takes a little more time to set up, but once it is built, it runs automatically, 24 hours a day, 365 days a week.

Consider the time clock. For many years, clocking in was a manual process done on paper. The team member needed to remember to write down when they started, when they took a break, and ended work.. Then they needed to remember to turn in the sheets at the end of the week. Someone then needed to manually input those hours into a computer system, which would many times have errors. Now, we have team members log in from their phone, or sometimes automatically when they arrive at a job. That data is transferred to the cloud and then synced with the accounting software that does payroll. Everything can be streamlined.

In most areas of our businesses, we have developed or purchased software that creates efficiency through automation. For example, we use:

- Fleet software for tracking our vehicles. We have installed dash cameras with artificial intelligence that tracks distracted driving. We generate a weekly report and videos of the people who are the most distracted drivers. This has saved us hundreds of thousands of dollars.

- Equipment tracking software. We have software that tracks our equipment through GPS.

- Job management software to monitor project progression and timelines.

- Marketing software to attract, capture, nurture, and follow up with potential customers. Most of this is completely automated.

- HR software to track time-clocking, HR tasks, automatic emails to team members, 401k data, etc.

- Training. For one of our companies, we have automated the sales process so people can watch well-crafted videos that take them through the whole sales process.

When is it time to automate?

- When you realize a process is inefficient: it takes too many people or wastes time and resources to complete a task.

- When details are getting missed. If you continually have team members miss important details, it's time to find a way to automate or systemize those processes.

- When you want to improve profits through efficiency.

What specific areas of your business need to be automated?

I immediately began to evaluate how well we were doing in all the aspects of being process-driven. We were already good at using technology to run our business, but I identified even more places it could be implemented. Further, I recognized that we had a few salespeople and technicians that in a sense held the keys to the kingdom when it came to their specific craft and roles in our company.

I was impressed with their A-player responses when I asked them to document their high-level processes so others could learn from them. I also acknowledged them for doing so, and made sure they felt honored for bringing their elite knowledge and skills to the company. I built them up with genuine gratitude for their contributions and willingness to raise our company's level of performance. In doing so, I realized again that top performers want to share what they know, especially when it is recognized. They want to feel that what they have taken the time to skillfully develop is being valued.

We had just finished remodeling our dream home, and a new energy had come over me as I envisioned the future of our family life and company. We had the perfect setup, living about ten minutes away from the office, and things were looking brighter every day. Jessica was pleased with my decision to keep the company, although I did not anticipate how she was about to test me in a major way.

One night after our boys were asleep, Jessica began to tell me what was on her mind. "I am sincerely grateful everything is coming together in such a big way. Skylar, you know my dream has always been to live at the beach. I think we should move to the beach," Jessica said without warning.

"But it's an hour away from the office, and we're only ten minutes away right now!" I replied, hoping she wasn't serious.

"You're a smart guy, babe, you can figure out how to make it work. That is one of the reasons I married you," she said, leaving me no escape. "And by the way, I think we should do it next month."

Jessica was always challenging me to do things that I didn't think were possible—which, when I got over myself, was certainly one of the reasons I admired her. I was not one to be comfortable being comfortable, so I immediately rejected the voice in my head saying, "*This won't work*", and focused on how to make it happen.

Joe had made a big shift in his company when he decided to hire a general manager to handle all the major functions of the company. That was my solution! But who would I hire to fill such a major role? There is so much to know, and our new culture had to be upheld with precision. Maybe there was someone in the company already that could step up to that role?

I sat at the kitchen table, glaring at the night sky through our large windows, and adjusted my power question to, "Who is the one person who would be the best fit as our general manager?" It didn't take long for the obvious answer to come. It was undoubtedly Melissa, our current operations manager.

I wasted no time. Within a week I had called Melissa in to extend the promotion to general manager. I could tell she was surprised, and she also recognized that she would have to increase her capacity as a leader. However, she gracefully accepted and agreed to develop herself even more. I copied off some key pages in the CEO's guidebook to give her some reference points of how I was developing my capacity as well, and to help her understand the clear direction of the company. No one I could find externally could match Melissa's commitment to our company. She bleeds Superior Restoration. She is the company's #1 cheerleader, and everyone knows it.

Right after my meeting with Melissa, I phoned Joe and told him the actions I had taken, and that apparently, we were now preparing to move to the beach. He suggested we postpone our next meeting until I got the move organized, and then we could pick them up again.

I considered myself to be somewhat adventurous, so four weeks later we had packed up all our things from our newly remodeled dream home, moved them into storage, and relocated to a small rental house on the water at Newport Beach.

The first couple of weeks of living an hour away from my office were not too bad. By the eighth week of driving into the office daily, something had to change. I considered myself to be a "life by design" kind of guy, and this was not working. I also regarded myself as very efficient and spending that much time driving was not productive for me. I needed to design myself out of this daily commute. I wondered how I would be able to either move my business closer to our new beach home or spend fewer days coming into the office.

Moving my office was not an ideal option, because my team all lived fairly close, and I did not want them to have to commute just for me. The second option would be going to the office less, which historically ended in my team having some dysfunction and me needing to come in to put out some fires. I did not care for either option, so I reluctantly continued the commute.

During my drive one day, I had an "aha moment." I was reading a book that had just described Parkinson's Law: "Work expands so as to fill the time available for its completion." It got me thinking. Did I really need five days a week to complete everything I need to do? With Melissa and the management team taking care of so many of the company leadership functions, many days I left early. I wondered how much time I wasted. *Could I really get everything done in two days a week?* After all, that was the vision, wasn't it?

I committed myself to go for it and start driving into the office three days a week to see if I could make it work. Otherwise, I would seriously have to relent and move back closer to the office.

REVIEW AND EVALUATIONS OF LESSONS LEARNED

Circle your current, honest answer.
1 = Not at All and 5 = Always

My business is process-driven as opposed to people-driven.

| 1 | 2 | 3 | 4 | 5 |

I have my processes documented utilizing SOP's.

| 1 | 2 | 3 | 4 | 5 |

As the leader, I follow the processes and do not deviate.

| 1 | 2 | 3 | 4 | 5 |

For any answer that is not a
5, what specific actions can you take to improve?

_____

_____

_____

_____

CHAPTER 15

PLAN

I spent a good part of the year coming into the office only three days a week, and to my surprise, everything seemed to be working fine. Our culture was stronger than it had ever been, our team was happy and performing well, and profit was growing. Then my fairly new general manager, Melissa, approached me—and did not think everything was working fine.

"We need to talk," Melissa started, with some animosity in her voice. She came into my office unannounced and closed the door.

"Sure. What's on your mind, Melissa?"

"Skylar, we see that you are receiving direction from your coach and mentor, but to be candid, our leaders here at Superior Restoration, me included, feel a huge lack of direction from you. I know you trust me and think I can handle being the general manager, but I have to be honest and tell you I am feeling overwhelmed with everything, and especially feeling like I have to come up with where to guide everyone," Melissa courageously confessed.

Instead of answering her immediately or reacting to the situation, as was my previous pattern, I sat silent for a moment and contemplated what the best solution would be. Then it dawned on me that instead of coming up with the solution myself, I would let Melissa come up with it. I wanted to create more of a solutions-focused company and culture, and this was a great opportunity to start.

"Thanks for sharing this with me, Melissa. I can definitely appreciate where you're coming from. What do you suggest we do to improve this situation?" I asked.

She gazed at me, a little surprised that I had put the matter right back into her lap. But I was right: she had already been thinking about possible solutions. "How about you consult with your coach on what he would do in this situation? In fact, I'm sure we would all love to meet him and learn from him as well," Melissa suggested.

I nodded my head in agreement and swallowed my pride a little, realizing I needed to learn some additional leadership skills for my team to feel clear on our vision.

That same day, I reached out to Joe. I relayed the conversation and Melissa's suggestion for him to come speak to our team.

"Well, I thought you would never ask," Joe said in an enthusiastic tone. "Melissa is feeling what many managers feel where there is no direction from the CEO. This is why it is absolutely true what it says in Proverbs: 'Where there is no vision, the people perish.'"

Joe agreed to come and do a strategy session with Melissa and my key leaders, and it proved to be exactly what we needed. His approach was simple and focused on the importance of setting our targets or goals and being held accountable consistently.

Joe's outline on providing direction and vision for our team:

- Identify one to three long-term goals for the next two to five years of the company.

- Break down the long-term goals into annual goals.

- Break down annual goals into quarterly goals for each manager.

- Create a consistent weekly leadership meeting to review everyone's progress on their quarterly goals. This keeps the focus and direction top of mind every week, with little room for error.

After a couple of months of taking action on Joe's strategy session, our team was in alignment. They felt very clear on our direction and they were solving their own problems. I decided to give Joe a call to tell him the good news of me being able to operate as the CEO only three days a week.

"I think I can go one day a week and everything will be fine, Joe!" I said with a high level of confidence.

Joe was not as convinced. "Skylar, while I think that it is fantastic that you have been able to operate three days a week for some time, I think that there is still some more work to do before you go to one day a week. You don't have the full system in place yet. I only know this is a premature idea because I've done it before. Sure, you can walk away from the business, and it can run temporarily without you. However, something will almost inevitably happen that pulls you back into the business. You have a machine that is 75% built."

While I did not want to hear it, I had come to trust that The CEO knew what he was talking about.

Joe continued, "The goal is to get the business to a place where it actually grows, not just operates, while you are away. Does that make sense?"

"Of course. I'm on board to make this happen the right way. I'm ready to meet again to take the next steps in my training."

"Actually, let's do it right now, over the phone," Joe said, and then started, ready or not. "The next step would be to read the final part of the Four Pillars System, which is the Plan section in my guidebook. You can have the people in place, a good product, and a good process, but if you don't have an executable plan to get you where you want to go, you will not get there. Execution is critical in any business. Many businesses have good ideas but struggle with executing at a high level. You must master goal setting, metrics, financials, and setting a clear vision. This way, your team has a clear path to follow even when you are not there. The Plan becomes the supervisor of key functions of the business, not you."

Goal-setting

Having clearly defined goals is critical for you and for your team. While this might seem like a basic skill, I have discovered that many of the business owners I work with are not crystal clear on their goals. They have a general idea of their intended direction, but their goals are not written down and their team members often do not have access to them. For the last 10 years, I have set annual goals and then reverse-engineered them to weekly targets. This works for both personal and professional goals. I call this process reverse engineering your goals.

Collapsing Time Frames

How do you create more results in one year than most people would in three years? You collapse time frames. You execute on more impactful and strategic outcomes than your competitors do. While they are working on closing a deal, you are hiring a new salesperson to close deals. While they are hiring a new salesperson, you are designing a duplicatable process to train new salespeople.

You do this by applying focus. You focus on the most important activities—which are usually not the most urgent activities. Then you train your team to do this same thing. We start out by focusing on our long-term goals (three to five years). Then we reverse engineer those goals into annual goals, then quarterly goals, and then into monthly goals. We then focus on achieving monthly goals and tracking the progress of these goals. This is how you collapse time frames and produce massive results.

SMART Goals

Whenever you create goals, you can use the modified acronym SMART.

- Specific (Example: $2,000,000 in revenue.)
- Measurable (The $2,000,000 is measurable on a daily/weekly/monthly/quarterly basis.)
- Achievable (Think big, but not so big that you stop trying when you get off-track.)
- Relevant (Make sure these goals are in line with your ultimate vision.)
- Time-specific (Set a specific end date: $2M in revenue by December 31st.)

Annual Strategy Sessions

What do you want to accomplish this year in your business? Do you want to buy a building? Increase revenue? Increase profitability? Implement a new system or new software?

At the end of each year, I go somewhere beautiful (usually the beach), bring a pen and paper, turn off my phone, and start thinking. What do I want to accomplish next year? Who do I want to become? What do I want my business to look like? Start visualizing what you want your life to look like by the end of next year. Write down everything you want in your business.

Once you are clear on what you want to accomplish, set up a strategy session with your leadership team. Discuss your vision with them and see if they are in alignment. Get their buy-in. Then set one to three annual goals for your business that everyone inside your organization will focus on for that year.

When you are clear on these annual goals, start the reverse-engineering process.

Quarterly Targets

To achieve one of the annual goals, what benchmarks or targets do you need to achieve on a quarterly basis? Break down the annual goal into quarterly targets. These quarterly goals will be your primary focus during the year. (We use the term *targets* instead of *goals*. I believe targets hold more weight. A sniper is completely committed to hitting his *target*. Many times goals are just an idea that people go after until it gets hard. Then they give up.)

I recommend having a strategy session each quarter to review your quarterly targets. Did you achieve the targets? If not, why? If yes, time to celebrate!

Monthly Targets

Once the quarterly targets are set, figure out what you have to do on a monthly basis to hit that target. Some people plan out all three months; some go month by month. Example: If your quarterly target is 90 new clients, then your monthly target may be 30.

Or if your quarterly target is to build out your SOPs for the accounting department, your first monthly target may be to list out all of the SOPs that need to be created. The second month may be to finish 50% of the SOPs.

You will be surprised at the results that are created from this level of planning and focus. It will change your business if you are disciplined with it.

One-page Plan

It is critical to have a document outlining all of your top priorities and objectives. Most companies call this a Strategic Plan. Strategic planning documents used to be up to 100+ pages long. Not many people read them. What I have found to be the most effective is a *One-page Plan*. The simpler you can display the information, the better. Then, if needed, you can go into more detail in other documents. The goal is to take everything you've done in planning and refine it so it fits on one page. This one-page plan has our Core Values, our Vision, our long-term goals, annual goals, quarterly goals, and our critical number. Every employee in our company has access to this document and knows where our company is going and what we are working on.

The One-page Plan is a powerful document that allows your entire company to be in alignment. One of the biggest hindrances to the success of your team is their lack of engagement, which many times comes from a lack of alignment in vision, core values and goals. Involving your team in planning sessions and goal setting increases engagement. Show them how each of the quarterly goals ties into the annual goal, which ties into the three-year goal, which makes the company's vision a reality. This document helps accomplish this. Many CEOs and leaders carry this document with them everywhere. They refer to it often with their teams.

For a One-page Plan template, go to www.2dayceo.com/resources/tools/onepageplan

After one of the meetings, I sat down with Melissa and asked how she was doing. I could tell that she was excited and energized. "Skylar, having a clear direction on where we are going was very important to me, more than I had realized. I like working for you, but I need to know that I have a future. I need to know that I am growing and have a clear path."

After that conversation with Melissa, I made it a point to share the vision with her and the entire team regularly. She was not the only one who felt like this. The entire team wanted to know where we were going. They were all on the bus, but they hadn't known where the bus was headed.

Meeting Rhythms

About three years into running my business, I realized our team was out of alignment. There were issues that weren't being addressed because everyone was busy. These small issues eventually turned into significant issues, and we had some key team members leave. I realized that we needed a better way to stay in alignment and resolve issues, so we started doing a weekly manager's meeting, and we've been doing it ever since.

Your meeting rhythms are the heartbeat of your business. This is where all of the information flows through the veins of your business. These meetings are where issues are brought up and resolved. These meetings create efficiencies in your company and help you move faster. We use the word rhythms because they are not sporadic. These meetings must be very consistent. They have to be, or they will eventually cease to exist.

How often should you meet with your team? I've seen companies overdo this and underdo this. I have put together an outline of an ideal meeting rhythm for a company.

Daily Huddle

Having a daily huddle has been game-changing for our team. This can be done in person or virtually via phone or video conference. Each manager has a 5-to-15 minute huddle each day with their teams. (Each team should have no more than 10 to 12 people on it.) They ask three questions to each team member:

- What did you accomplish yesterday?
- What are you accomplishing today?
- What roadblocks do you foresee?

Don't spend time diving deep into every roadblock. You really just want to use this meeting to keep people on track and *focused on their top priorities*. You also want to be able to support them with any challenges they may have. This daily huddle creates great alignment and collaboration within teams. One person may need to go pick up some materials and another person may be driving that way. By communicating daily in this manner, you allow the team to collaborate and solve problems together.

Don't get tangled up in trying to fix something if it is going to take more than one minute. I see managers do this regularly, and the call ends up being 20 or 25 minutes long. This is not okay. People have jobs to go do and may grow weary of the daily huddles. Just call the person in need of additional support after wrapping up the huddle.

Weekly or Bi-monthly Team Meeting

These meetings are usually one hour. Review what is working and what is not, and any important topics that need to be discussed. We usually review the scoreboard and progress on top priorities.

Monthly Meetings

I like to do monthly meetings with the entire company. These are usually one hour and focus on inspiring the team. We talk about core values, recognize team members, hand out awards, and discuss any hot topics. The team really enjoys seeing each other at these meetings and the energy should be high.

Quarterly Planning Sessions

Each quarter, review the previous quarter's progress with your leadership/management team and plan for the next quarter.

I have included a free copy of this quarterly strategy session agenda at: www.2dayceo.com/resources

Annual Leadership Team Strategy Session

This is a very important meeting. Always have an annual strategy session to discuss how the year went: what worked, what did not, and what you are planning on doing differently next year. Set the vision for the year and get the team's buy-in on new annual goals.

After the annual strategy session with Joe, we had our goals clarified and our team in alignment. This weekly meeting to review the progress on our goals and our One-page Plan became the most important meeting of the week. In this one meeting, I was able to see all of the important progress and challenges within my company. This meeting became the only meeting that I did not miss.

For the following quarters, I ran a shorter version of the strategy session. I would go offsite with the management team and we would review the performance of the previous quarters. Some quarters were amazing and we hit most of our quarterly targets. Some quarters had very weak performance. We used this opportunity to review what didn't work and how we could do things differently. This regular course correction allowed us to become better and grow. If we didn't hit a target, I made a big deal of it. I wanted us to have a high standard of winning and avoid shrugging off losses.

As this weekly meeting became consistent and valuable, we decided to add a scoreboard that showed all of our KPIs and Metrics. I added all of the numbers that I thought were most important to track to this scoreboard. I wasn't a pro at this, so I got some advice from Joe on how to do it correctly.

Metrics and KPIs

A plane has dials and gauges to tell the pilot how it is doing. Imagine a plane with no gauges! Similarly, many businesses have no clue what their numbers are. They are flying blind. Your metrics and KPIs give you direct insight into how the business is doing. Are your sales on track? How about your accounts receivable? What about production? You must first get clear on what the most important numbers to track are and then become radically disciplined to track them on a regular basis.

What Is the Difference Between a Metric and KPI?

A metric is a number that you track to measure how well the company, or a process within the company, is doing. $2,000,000 in revenue is a metric.

KPI stands for Key Performance Indicator, and is a number that measures the success of a goal's outcome. For example, if you wanted to achieve the metric of $2,000,000, you might set a KPI for a number of sales meetings with prospects each quarter. The KPI would lead to achieving the $2M sales goal.

Lagging Indicators vs Leading Indicators

It's important to know the difference between a lagging and a leading indicator. Many people track lagging indicators. A lagging indicator might be revenue or net profit. However, what led to that number? This would be the leading indicator.

If your target was 30 sales a month and you only had 15 sales, you want to identify the cause of this. So you might start tracking the number of sales calls or the number of sales meetings with prospects. This number would be the leading indicator. You want to track leading indicators because they tell you how the business is doing before you get the final result. Once you know you had a bad month, it's hard to fix it. But if you were tracking the number of sales meetings each week, you would know they were lower than expected, and you could course-correct the following week.

Leading indicators allow you to course-correct quickly.

Who Should Be Assigned a KPI?

Everyone in your organization should have a KPI they are responsible to meet. For example, the customer service role can track the number of calls completed per day. The salesperson can track the number of new appointments set or the number of new meetings that week.

You want to assign a KPI to each person so they know what they are working towards. Many team members are unclear about what they are responsible for. They are just doing a job with no direction. Give them some direction by giving them a number that they can track and improve on weekly.

What Numbers Should You Track?

Here are some ideas of metrics and KPIs you can start tracking. I recommend creating your own based on the goals of your company.

- Number of new leads generated
- Number of sales calls
- Number of sales appointments completed
- Number of jobs completed or won
- Accounts Receivable dollars
- Accounts Receivable over 90 days

- Cash collections
- Number of customer complaints
- Number of safety incidents (auto or personal injury).
- Overtime hours as a percentage (%) of total hours worked
- Net Promoter Score (NPS) from customer satisfaction surveys
- Sales-closing ratio
- Liquidity ratio (ask your accountant)
- Revenue per employee (track monthly)
- Number of products sold or services completed
- Number of units produced

Ideally, you want to track these numbers on a weekly basis. Tracking them weekly allows you to course-correct faster. Also, you want to make sure that only one person "owns" a metric. Having more than one person responsible for the same metric creates a lack of accountability. If more than one person is accountable, no one is accountable.

We track these numbers on what we call a scoreboard. Some companies call it a flash report. We list out all of our key metrics and KPIs on this scoreboard. I am able to tell at a glance which parts of the business are suffering and which are thriving.

The Critical Number

There are so many things to track in any business. So what should you be tracking? Imagine that you can only track one number all year. This one number will give you a pulse on your business. What would that number be? This will be the number that you and your team track.

Now start tracking this number weekly. When you track it weekly, you will be able to see the trends.

Once you get clear on your critical number, find out what your second, third, fourth, and so on numbers would be. Start out with a few numbers and start adding them once you become comfortable with the process.

Best Practices with Scoreboards

Make sure scoreboards don't reflect numbers on your profit and loss statement/income statement. You want these numbers to be the drivers. Usually, they are activity-based numbers; for instance, the number of sales, number of phone calls, number of new products delivered, etc.

It took about two months for me to clarify all of our most important KPIs, metrics, and numbers. Once that was complete, it took another four months for our teams to become familiar with and truly know those numbers. As a result, something interesting happened. The team started to truly "own" their numbers and naturally became accountable for them. They made decisions based on those numbers. This process helped us to create new "standards" for our critical numbers, which led to us being able to instantly tell when a part of our company was underperforming. The scoreboard became one of our most valuable tools to operate the business.

During one of my meetings with Joe, he asked me to bring my financials. "Skylar, how often do you review your company's financials?" "Maybe once a quarter," I replied. "Once a quarter? That is not nearly often enough. I recommend doing a detailed review of your financials on a monthly basis." I pulled up my financials and realized that I didn't even know how to read them. I had just always looked at the "bottom line" to see if we were profitable or not. "Honestly, Joe, I really don't understand how to use these."

Joe replied, "Skylar, you need to review these consistently and understand how to read them. I recommend getting with your CPA immediately and having them teach you some of the basics. Once you do that, we can sit down to do a deep dive into how to use your financial statements to make business decisions. Most owners just look at their bottom line and never really use their statements to direct the company. I call this running the business based on the numbers."

The whole financial transparency thing really scared me. I was afraid my team would think I made too much money. I reached out to Joe and asked exactly how he did it, and copied his plan. Before I launched the plan, I held a company-wide meeting and asked everyone what they thought our company made in profit from every dollar. The resounding number was 50%. Fifty percent—I wish!

Initially, people were shocked that we were revealing our real financials. The numbers were lower than they had assumed, so it was an even easier transition. After a short period of time, I saw the engagement of our team increase. People were actively involved, wanting to know more about how the company ran so they could help improve the numbers. It was really working!

During that process, I started creating more reports so I could have better optics into the company. I had to do a decent amount of work to create the reports, but they gave me great visibility into each part of the business. I had most of our different software export data into Google Sheets, which allowed me to see all the data in one place. I then created a dashboard from all this data. I was starting to see the light at the end of the tunnel. Maybe businesses really could be systemized and operate without the owner.

Understanding your Financials

For a large part of my business career, I did not truly understand my financials. When I say financials, I am referring to the financial statements of a business. This includes the profit and loss statement (income statement), balance sheet, and statement of cash flow. You may have other statements you look at, but these are the ones that are most relevant to a majority of businesses.

Many entrepreneurs do not fully understand their financials, and therefore struggle to know how their business is really doing. They are months and sometimes weeks away from a cash-flow crisis. They are not operating effectively or efficiently. They look at their bank balance and think everything is all right. Or, even worse, they think the business is doing poorly when it really isn't. What you do not know will hurt you in business.

The upside of understanding your business financials is that you can adjust regularly and make your business more profitable. This is called running the business by the numbers. Most business professionals can look at a financial statement, see where there are inefficiencies, and know what dials to turn to improve the business. This should be your eventual goal as a business owner.

So, without being an accountant, what information should you be looking at and how often?

Financial statements to review:

- Profit & Loss (aka Income Statement or P&L)
- Balance Sheet
- Cashflow Statement (for medium to larger companies)

I am not going to go into depth on how to read these statements. Like Joe, my recommendation is that you ask your CPA for some of their time—spend the money—and have them teach you how to effectively read these statements. Ask them what numbers and ratios you should be looking at.

Here are a few tips:

- Understand how your profit and loss statement connects to your balance sheet.

- Make sure you include ratios on your financial statements. Just looking at the numbers will often not tell you what you need to know. The ratios give you more insight.

- Get financial statements on a monthly basis. Some businesses may need them more often, but a general rule of thumb is monthly.

- Set up a monthly meeting with your CPA or CFO to review the numbers with you.

- Spend time understanding your numbers, including your gross profit, gross margin, cost of goods sold, etc. Really understand what your numbers are telling you about your business. How much is your payroll each month? What about materials or manufacturing costs? You should know the important numbers in your business.

The Benefits of Financial Transparency

There is power in financial transparency—otherwise known as *open-book* management. Initially, I didn't want to share my numbers with my team. I thought they would think I made too much money. I thought they wouldn't understand the risk/reward tied to the business profitability, so I made sure my team never saw the full financial picture. What I found out later was that my team actually thought I made more profit than I did. Since they never saw the finances, they thought we were always raking in the cash.

I read a book called *The Great Game of Business*, and it brought up a valid argument. How do I expect to get my team to make business decisions on their own if they don't even know how those decisions affect our profitability? I had given my team almost full autonomy to make decisions, but I never shared the financial impact of their decisions. They only knew half the picture.

After reading that book, I decided to put together a plan to share my business financials with the team. It took about four months and a lot of strategic planning, but eventually, I rolled out a plan and started sharing my numbers weekly with all of my team members. This plan also included a bonus plan for all team members if we hit profit goals. This was the first time we offered bonuses for everyone—from trainee to GM—based on how the company did. This bonus was proportionate to their wages. This changed the game for us.

Interestingly enough, as we became more transparent, our team started to trust the company more. They started to understand how their decisions affected everything, from overtime hours to how much we spent on coffee every month. After a year, our team knew most of the line item expenses on our P&L statement intimately. Not only were we transparent with our numbers, but our team was bonused based on the profitability of our company. This created an incredible buy-in and engagement from our team. Our engagement has never been higher.

The first two years that we ran open-book management, our company operating profit increased by almost 50% each year. To be clear, I am not saying to immediately share all of your financials with the team. This must be done strategically if you decide to do it. If you want higher engagement and a team that can run your business, this may be an important piece of the puzzle.

REVIEW AND EVALUATIONS OF LESSONS LEARNED

Circle your current, honest answer.
1 = Not true at all and 5 = Completely true

My team is clear on where we are going as a company and can recite it.

1   2   3   4   5

I have a clear direction on where we are going.
I have annual goals in writing.

1   2   3   4   5

I have a deep understanding of my financials and review them regularly.

1   2   3   4   5

For any answer that is not a 5,
what specific actions can you take to improve?

_____

_____

_____

_____

PART THREE

FINAL EXECUTION

My habit of waking up early was being rewarded with all the processes and systems I had been able to implement. One particularly beautiful morning, I decided to take a walk on the beach while it was still dark, just before the sunrise. With the clouds sporadically spread out on the horizon, I could sense it was going to be a brilliant display of God's handiwork. I suddenly had the urge to have my family next to me to witness the radiant sunrise, so I ran a couple blocks back home. I knew they would be asleep, but this was worth waking up for. I picked up our youngest son, Jeremiah, and gently told our oldest son, Brenden, to get up and put on some sandals.

"Where are we going, Dad?" Brenden asked.

"We are going to the beach to watch the sunrise," I answered.

I laid the still-sleeping Jeremiah on our couch and slipped into our bedroom and whispered to Jessica, "Hey babe, c'mon, let's go watch the sunrise. It's beautiful out there."

Jessica came to consciousness and said, "What about the boys? We can't just leave them here."

"They're coming, too. I already woke them up, they're in the front room," I responded.

Soon we were all on the beach with our bare feet in the cool sand. Jeremiah didn't want to walk and was still wrestling with waking up, so I just held him. Jessica brought a blanket for us to sit on as we took in the majesty of the sun rising above the calm ocean water. The clouds lit up and looked like they were on fire. We were silent as we listened to the waves crash over and over again. I looked down at Jeremiah, who was now awake and entranced by the magnificently colored sky. I glanced over at Jessica, who had her arms around Brenden. She sensed me looking at her and couldn't help but smile back. I leaned her way, indicating that I wanted a special sunrise kiss, which I received. Few words were spoken, but a whole lot of things were being said just by us being together, practically all alone, on the beach close to our house.

A string of thoughts began to engulf me. We had actually spontaneously moved to the beach and enjoyed countless sunsets, sunrises, and romantic walks together. Not everything was perfect, but we somehow figured it out. We were not just creating cherished memories—we were living our dreams, one day at a time. As I was taking in the beauty of the new morning with my precious family and thinking of my many blessings, a quote from Henry David Thoreau came to my mind. "The mass of men lead lives of quiet desperation, and go to the grave with the song still in them."

I felt like I had escaped any possibility of quiet desperation. My music was all out there, all the time. I had been working tirelessly to implement everything The CEO had coached me on over the past three years, and was now only going into the office three days a week. I knew we were so close to achieving the status of a 2-Day-CEO, and I felt ready to execute on whatever I was lacking. It was time to reach out to Joe again—but only after fully taking in the divine morning at the beach with my family.

After exchanging some pleasantries over the phone, The CEO started off, "Skylar, you have successfully implemented the foundation to have the team and the processes that have been built to run without you. The last section in my guidebook will outline how to effectively step out of the business most days. I am going to give you 90 days to implement it, and then our next meeting will be at our house. Karen has been reminding me often that we would love to have you, Jessica, and the boys over for dinner. So go make this happen and we'll see you in three months."

With The CEO's guidebook in hand, I dove into the remaining material. Everything I had implemented so far had proven to be worth its weight in gold. I'm not going to say it's been totally easy to put into action; however, I can confidently say it has been 100% worth the effort. I have honestly just trusted the process, and the rewards have been plentiful.

How to Step Away

Dedicate specific days to your company.

Fit as much in as you can on the days you are at the company. Remember Parkinson's Law: Work expands to fill the time allotted. If you allot three or four days, you will be surprised by how much you can get done within that period.

Start by only going to the office four days a week, and then reduce from there.

Be aware of the time you spend outside of the office working. You can easily bring your work home and have it take up your family time. Don't do that. Set a specific time each day that you "knock off for the day" and stop working: 4:00 p.m., 5:00 p.m., or whatever works for you best.

Explain the plan to your team.

Share with the team that you believe in them and you want to start giving them more responsibility. Share that your goal is to eventually have them run and grow the company, which will mean more opportunities for them. Also, give them clarity on which days you will be coming into the office.

Meet with your team weekly. Dedicate time to the most important team members that you need to stay connected to. Set a meeting at the same time and day every week. *Do not miss your own meetings!* If you miss meetings, your team will miss them also.

Have a set agenda for these meetings, and make sure you discuss all the hot topics. Try to avoid your team coming to you during the week with issues. Have them add any issues to the agenda for your weekly meeting.

Stop solving problems.

Part of getting your team to operate without you is to stop solving all of their problems. When they come to you with issues or challenges or need help with decisions, ask them "What do you think?" or "How would you handle that?" I ask this question to my general manager whenever she brings issues to me. The only way they learn is by allowing them to fail and learn from their mistakes.

There will be times when a team member presents a solution you don't think is best. If their idea is detrimental to the business, step in and explain why you think it should be done a certain way. However, if it is not, allow the team member to make the decision.

Create a decision matrix.

Identify what decisions team members have the ability to make on their own. Be very clear and explicit about this. How much can they spend without approval? Are they allowed to change processes without your approval? Can they fire a team member without you knowing? Are they able to change branding or your goals without you?

Start actively reviewing your scoreboard and reports.

Never take your eye off the ball. Make sure you are always checking these reports and scoreboards to verify the accuracy of the numbers. Over time, some reports and numbers will become outdated or inaccurate; update them.

Stay involved in the hiring process for key team members.

Although you have documented the hiring process by now, you do not want your team to accidentally hire someone who could be cancerous to your organization. It is also important that you have relationships with your new team members, especially if they are in critical roles.

Stay emotionally connected to your team.

Put a process in place for you to go to breakfast or lunch with different team members on days you are at the office. Ask how people are doing. Let them know you still care even though you are there less. Always remain engaged with your team members.

CEO Optics

As you are stepping away from your business, the reports you look at become even more important. Just because you are not at the office or talking with the team daily does not mean you don't need to have your finger on the pulse. You must know how your business is doing on a week-by-week basis.

Find a way to turn anything that is important inside your company into a report or number. Review these on a weekly or monthly basis. These are the areas that you want to look at regularly.

Scoreboard with key metrics

You should have all of your key metrics and critical numbers in one place. We use the term *scoreboard*. This scoreboard gives me all the data I need at a glance to know how the company is doing.

Ideally, you want to track these numbers on a weekly basis. Reviewing them weekly allows you to course-correct faster. Also, you want to make sure that only one person "owns" a metric. Having more than one person responsible creates a lack of accountability. *If more than one person is accountable, no one is accountable.*

Core process reports

What core processes run your business? For each core process, find a way to easily see how that process is operating on a weekly basis. Is the process running well or is the output of that process broken? What number/metric/report will tell you if the process is effectively working or not?

Once you are clear on those core processes, put them on a spreadsheet with the link to the specific report. Open the spreadsheet once a month to verify that all of your core processes are working correctly.

For example, we have fleet software that lists all of the company vehicles, including a lot of detail about those vehicles and their drivers. I created a key report that shows me gas usage, utilization of vehicles, miles driven, number of speeding violations, etc.— basically, all of the data I want to glance at every month to see if anything stands out that needs to be corrected. I set up a basic fleet dashboard that shows me all of this data at a glance. Now, if I notice that we are getting speeding violations regularly, that means one of our processes may not be working (our fleet manager checking in regularly with the drivers).

Whatever you track improves! If there is a specific thing in your business that is not doing well, start tracking it and reporting on it weekly, and you will see progress made.

Scorecards and snapshot reports/dashboards will give you the insight that you need to be able to see if anything is off track within your company.

Financial reports

Review your bank accounts on a regular basis (daily or weekly). I still personally sign all of our checks (we use digital checks, so I can do it remotely). I press a couple of buttons, and everything is signed. I do this because I want to keep an eye on the funds going out and want the team to know that I am still watching. I am still engaged. The highest chance for embezzlement occurs when your team knows that you are not engaged or watching.

My general manager and accounting team review all of the checks and confirm that the amounts are correct. I then get a report of everything getting paid that week. I review it and spot-check invoices. Then I sign the checks.

I review our credit card and bank statements monthly.

Monthly financials

I review our monthly profit and loss, balance sheet, and statement of cash flows on a monthly basis with our accounting manager and GM.

Accounts receivable and payable reports

I get weekly reports on the AR/AP of the company, along with cash flow reports.

As you are reviewing these, you may realize that there are important reports that you need to pay attention to. Every business is different.

People and Culture

I don't have a computer at the office. Actually, I don't even have a desk anymore and haven't for a couple of years. I am not at the office to get tasks done. If I am only in the office two days a week (or less), I want to make sure I am meeting with the team and involved in all important meetings. Emails and tasks can be done remotely. The first thing I do every morning is greet every person in the office. I connect with them and see how they are doing. I do this by asking about their lives and asking what support they need.

One of the most important areas to keep a close eye on is your team's morale. As previously mentioned, *micromanage your culture.* When you notice morale is low, attend to it immediately. A way to check in with morale is to have conversations with your team members. I usually go on "walk and talks" around the office to see what is going on in people's lives and how their attitude is. When I sense that their morale or attitude is off, I ask questions to see where the problem is. Then I provide some coaching to help them mentally move through it. Low engagement reduces productivity and increases problems.

Another way to keep an eye on culture and people without being there is to send out a quarterly engagement survey. A well-drafted survey will give you insight into how engaged your team members are.

I have included a copy of one that you can use here:
www.2dayceo.com/resources

After you have systemized your business and have it running like a well-oiled machine, a common challenge may arise, such as having a key team member leave. This will likely require you to come back into the business for a short period of time. Sometimes this is inevitable. However, if you pay close attention to the details of team member morale and culture, you can prevent people from leaving or becoming disengaged. If you really care about your team, it will show. If you don't, that will show as well.

It took every bit of the 90 days Joe had allotted me to put the steps of Final Execution into place. I knew I had to overcome my apprehension of only showing up two days a week and demonstrate my full trust in my people to run the company without me being there every day. It was the only way to see if the processes and systems that were now in place were working. Although not everything was perfect, we had a very productive 90 days, and our sales and production were better than when

I was at the office every single day. Not only that, but I also observed how empowered my team felt to make it happen without me.

What I was most surprised by was how my team stepped up, and how happy they were. They really enjoyed running the business. Even though I was there for only two days a week, I was working on the business those days. The team handled everything related to the production of the business. Our engagement was off the charts. Team members were working later, engaging with each other through our company-wide chat app, and their attitudes were noticeably improved.

On one of my days in the office, I was with the management team during our weekly meeting. Melissa pulled up her computer and showed me our most recent customer survey scores. "Skylar, this is the highest score we have ever had on these surveys. We've had fewer customer complaints with everything that has been put into place. The team is really striving to do their best, and I am truly excited to be a part of this organization. Thank you for trusting me and our team to get it done."

It was a proud moment as I responded, "Of course! It's been worth the effort. I love seeing everyone so engaged."

Melissa continued with excitement, "Last week, three of our new hires came to us and said they have never worked for a company that cared so much. Each one stated this is the best job they have ever had."

I gave the management team a huge smile. "I just wanted to thank all of you for being such incredible team players and really caring about the company. You embody every part of our core values," I complimented, as they smiled ear to ear.

The much-anticipated evening finally arrived for my family to have dinner with Joe's at his southern California house. I have to admit there were a lot of feelings on the surface surrounding the whole event. I was excited, nervous, happy, and a bit emotional all at the same time. It had been a few years since I had been to his house, but this is where it had all started over 15 years ago. I don't know why, but at the last minute, I grabbed my now well-worn *Lessons Learned from The CEO* notebook and put it in the car to take with us. Maybe it was just out of habit in hopes that The CEO would share another nugget of knowledge.

Karen greeted us warmly at the door and wanted to hold three-year-old toddler Jeremiah from the moment she laid eyes on him. Her boys, Joey and Jeremy, were all grown up and she missed holding little ones. No grandkids had come yet, but she did relate that both of their boys had married wonderful girls and were doing very well. Interestingly enough, they were both CEOs of two individual companies Joe had helped them start. This family had truly created a real legacy of leaders.

Joe insisted on telling the story of how we first met. Thankfully, Brenden was too young to understand that his dad had unlawfully broken into Joe's restaurant, and just thought it was funny that I would enter through a hatch door on the roof instead of the front door. I suppose he will find out someday what really happened.

We had a very pleasant dinner and moved to the family room. Karen was still holding our youngest as he was drifting off to sleep when Joe asked, "Skylar, did you by chance bring your *Lessons Learned* notebook?"

I was grateful I had followed my instincts and went out to the car to retrieve it. Once back inside, Joe asked me to give it to him. "Skylar, when you were here many years ago and we were working through the power of core values and culture, I glanced at the inside cover of your notebook. I was truly impressed with what I saw you wanted your future to look like, and I admit that I even said a simple little prayer that this would come true for you. It has been quite the journey for you, my friend. Karen, would you mind reading what Skylar wrote here as a 15-year-old boy?" Joe asked. He handed the notebook to Karen in exchange for Jeremiah, who was now sound asleep.

Although she did not want to give up holding our son, she gracefully complied and slowly read the contents I had written shortly after meeting The CEO, when he agreed to mentor me as a young man.

1. I will be a successful CEO of a company with many team members that love working for me and want to follow me, just like Joe.
2. I will have a hot wife and kids I spend time with.
3. I will create a life of massive success by helping others.

Karen had to pause a couple of times as she became visibly emotional, knowing I had accomplished everything I had written all those years ago. Jessica and I were both overcome with tears of gratitude—gratitude for all of the trying experiences that shaped us, and gratitude especially for Joe, who graciously decided to mentor a young man who could have easily sunk into a very different, destructive path in life. It was easy to recognize that Joe not only changed my life, but changed the entire path of our family and future generations.

With my oldest boy, Brenden, on my lap, I glanced at Jessica, tenderly put my arm around her, and pulled her close to me. Then I peered over at the man I owed so much to. I smiled through my tears and mouthed the words, "Thank you!"

Still holding our sleeping little boy, Joe nodded gently, acknowledging my gratitude. He just sat there in silence for a long period of time with a pleasant smile on his face, letting us all take in the moment.

Suddenly, I felt a tangible shift and realization occur inside of me. For my entire life, I had been trying to prove that I was good enough—to validate that I was significant and important—when in reality, deep down inside of me all that really mattered was my family and the unconditional love I had for them. I felt the constant necessity of having to prove myself instantly melt away into the truth that I was born good enough, and so is every human being. I smiled at the fact that it took this rollercoaster of a journey to come to this realization, and confirmed in my mind once again, "Yes, everything happens *for us* and *for our good.*"

Before we left Joe and Karen's house, The CEO told me that the day would come when I would find a bigger objective in life than just business. He said being a 2-Day-CEO would eventually facilitate a passion for a higher purpose. I did not know what that fully meant at the moment, but I trusted that in time it would come to fruition.

EPILOGUE

It has been over five years since I transitioned to two days a week at Superior Restoration. The last two of those years, since COVID-19 hit, I have been working in the business a total of one day per week. To top it off, five months ago, we decided to move our entire family from California, where I have lived all my life, to Dallas, Texas. Our team at Superior Restoration (which is still located in California) has been running the entire business with limited involvement from me. Since moving to Texas, I have been involved in one virtual hour-long meeting per week with my executive team. What I have realized through this whole process is that they have it handled. They really don't need me. When you hire competent people and give them the tools to succeed, you will be surprised at what they are capable of.

Over the last year, I have been able to work on the things I am most passionate about, which happens to be coaching other business owners to do the same thing I was able to do. With all my extra time, I have created a system called The Four Pillar Framework, based on the 2-Day-CEO model, that allows owners to systemize their business. My team of coaches and I are spending the next phase of our lives pouring our effort into others to help them get where they want to go. The icing on the cake is that my team at Superior Restoration has found more fulfillment, fun, and passion than they ever would have if I was the one telling them what to do and micromanaging them. This has been a true win/win!

Why did I decide to write this book and share my story? I share this because I want you to know what is possible. I want you to think BIG. The world is waiting for you to step up into your greatness. There is no better time than now to take action. Cheers to an incredible life of Liberty and Impact!

FINAL THOUGHTS

At the beginning of this book, I mentioned that life is not about what you acquire, but rather the impact you make on the lives around you, and who you become during the journey of life.

What will you do with your time while here on this earth? Will you build a business that makes a difference in the people who work there? Will your business positively impact the people it comes into contact with? Who are you becoming on this journey of being an entrepreneur, and do you like the person you are seeing in the mirror?

As I have associated with many other business owners throughout the years, I often saw the struggle of balancing their faith, family, and fitness with their business. I felt called to support men, as I can relate with them the most. I wanted them to avoid the challenges of being too out of balance and the damage it can cause to their family and their health. The divorce rate in our country is rising. Many fathers are absent and not present at home. Anxiety and depression are the main reasons people visit the hospital now. All of these are major problems. The businessmen I knew struggled to effectively scale their business, which led to sacrificing their health and their relationships with their wives and kids. The irony was that they did this all in the hopes of building a business that would allow them *more* time with their family. In reality, it was creating irreparable damage to the ones they loved most.

So, as is the case for many great solutions, out of my personal struggles rose a solution. I have spent the last five years developing a program for married businessmen to reach their full potential in their faith, family, fitness, and finance. I call these the Four Pillars. I have found that if men can learn to invest in these pillars on a regular basis, they will be more fulfilled, and it will create more harmony at home.

After multiple iterations and working with hundreds of men, Rise Up Kings was born. Rise Up Kings is now one of the fastest-growing faith-based business programs to help men learn the tools they need to grow in their faith, family, fitness, and finance. Our motto has become *When you change a man, you change the world!* The world needs men who lead their families and businesses well.

You can visit www.RiseUpKings.com for more information on how you or someone you know can be a part of this life-changing movement.

2-Day-CEO Coaching and Peer Groups

The journey of an entrepreneur can be a lonely one, with many valleys. Many business owners have never learned how to properly build and scale a business. Even those who went to school for this still struggle in today's marketplace. I understand this at my core and have developed a peer program for business owners to help them scale their companies. If you want to align yourself with other business owners who are utilizing the 2-Day-CEO system, I've provided the links below.

To learn about CEO Peer Groups or our one-on-one business coaching, visit www.2dayceo.com/coaching

I know how valuable your time is, so THANK YOU for spending it with me. I hope my story and guidebook have been very valuable to you, and have given you the inspiration, mindset, and tools to build something great.

Skylar Lewis

ACKNOWLEDGEMENTS

I would like to acknowledge:

- My Lord and Savior Jesus Christ, for the life he has allowed me to live and the lives I've been able to impact.

- My wife, Jessica, for continuing to push me to be the man I am today. Whenever I want to quit or take the easy road, she always challenges me to be more.

- All of my mentors, coaches, and consultants that have poured into my life.

- My great friend Thomas Blackwell who supported me on this book.

- The team members at each of my businesses who have been there through the highs and lows.

ABOUT THE AUTHOR

Skylar Lewis started his journey to become a 2-Day-CEO while in his teens. Since then, he has created several multi-million dollar companies and employs dozens of team members in different industries. Skylar is the founder of Rise Up Kings and 2DayCeo, and his passion is coaching and speaking to business owners on how to rise up and live a life of liberty and fulfillment. To request Skylar as a coach or speaker, go to www.2dayceo.com/resources

CEO COACHING

- ▶ Have a master coach show you the ropes in business.
- ▶ Learn from people who have done it before.
- ▶ Take the fast track to success.

Go to
WWW.2DAYCEO.COM/COACHING

RISE UP KINGS

EVENTS AND MASTERMINDS

Join one of the fastest faith-based business communities for men who want to improve their Faith, Family, Fitness, and Finances.

Faith

Family

Fitness

Finance

FOLLOW
SKYLAR LEWIS

I am always giving out free tips, tools and strategies to help you scale your business!

GO TO
WWW.2DAYCEO.COM/SOCIAL
TO FIND MY PROFILES:

AND CHECK OUT OUR PODCAST
WWW.RISEUPKINGS.COM/PODCAST